THOMAS JEFFERSON AND THE CREATION OF AMERICA

DOUGLAS T. MILLER

☑®

Facts On File, Inc.

Thomas Jefferson and the Creation of America

Facts On File, Inc.
11 Penn Plaza
New York NY 10001

Library of Congress Cataloging-in-Publication Data

Miller, Douglas T.
  Thomas Jefferson and the creation of America / Douglas T. Miller.
    p.   cm. — (Makers of America)
  Includes bibliographical references (p.   ) and index.
  ISBN 0-8160-3393-5
  1. Jefferson, Thomas, 1743–1826. 2. Presidents—United States—
Biography. I. Title. II. Series: Makers of America (Facts on
File, Inc.)
  E332.M65   1997
  973.4′6′092—dc21
  [B]   96–29803

Facts On File books are available at special discounts when purchased in bulk quantities for businesses, associations, institutions, or sales promotions. Please call our Special Sales Department in New York at 212/967-8800 or 800/322-8755.

You can find Facts On File on the World Wide Web at
http://www.factsonfile.com

Text design by Cathy Rincon
Cover design by Matt Galemmo

Printed in the United States of America

MP FOF 10 9 8 7 6 5 4 3 2 1

This book is printed on acid-free paper.

CONTENTS

To Sus,
Bellis, Tilly, and Fanny
The Women of the Dobie Manor

Thomas Jefferson invented the swivel chair. He also devised the U.S. decimal system of coinage; an improved plow; and the grid pattern for laying out the nation's cities, counties, and states. He authored the Declaration of Independence, laws for the establishment of religious freedom and public support for education, an ordinance barring slavery in the territories north of the Ohio River, and a book on the state of Virginia. During the American Revolution, he served in the Continental Congress, the Virginia legislature, and as that state's governor. In the post-Revolutionary period, he was appointed as minister to France and Washington's secretary of state. Elected to the vice presidency in 1796, in 1800 and again in 1804, voters selected him as the third president of the United States. In retirement he founded the University of Virginia and carried on a remarkable correspondence with his former political rival John Adams. Incredibly, both Jefferson and Adams died on July 4, 1826, the 50th anniversary of the Declaration of Independence.

Jefferson represents the summit of the Enlightenment in America and helped embody the spirit of the Enlightenment in creating a nation conceived in liberty and dedicated to the proposition that all men are created equal. He articulated the dreams of everyday people and promoted a literal reading of such phrases as "natural rights" and "popular sovereignty." Americans cherish George Washington as the father of their country and celebrate Abraham Lincoln as the martyr who held the nation together through the trials of the Civil War; but it is Thomas Jefferson who personifies the country's highest ideals—liberty and equality. How fitting then that these

three leaders are the only presidents memorialized with monuments that grace the Tidal Basin of Washington, D.C.

Jefferson was amazingly versatile. In addition to being
arguably the most prominent political figure of the Revolutionary War generation, he was also the nation's foremost
architect, landscape designer, educational theorist, and connoisseur of fine wines. He further stood out as an eminent
scientist and inventor, an accomplished violinist, a skilled
linguist, a good lawyer, a serious mathematician, an amateur
anthropologist, and a gourmet vegetarian with a particular
liking for peas.

As much as any individual in American history, the author
of the Declaration of Independence deserves the designation
"Maker of America." *Thomas Jefferson and the Creation of
America* aims to bring this fascinating figure alive for a new
generation of readers. More than any other Revolutionary
leader, Jefferson had a vision of what America should stand
for. His principles and ideals gave coherence to the new nation.
Just as Jefferson spoke to the aspirations of ordinary citizens
in his day, his ideals of liberty, equality, natural rights, and
self-government are just as relevant to the world of today.

Douglas T. Miller

CREATING AMERICA

Late in December 1775, the 32-year-old Thomas Jefferson, worried about his family's safety, hurriedly left Philadelphia. Accompanied by his servant Bob, he began the arduous weeklong horseback ride to his home in Virginia. Tall and lanky with reddish hair, freckled face, and hazel eyes, Jefferson was a member of the Virginia delegation to the Continental Congress. Representing the 13 English North American colonies, the Continental Congress had been attempting to deal with the deepening conflict between the colonies and Great Britain.

On April 19, 1775, fighting had erupted in Lexington and Concord, Massachusetts, and through the remainder of the year war raged between rebel colonists and English redcoats (as they were called for the color of their uniforms). That June, the Continental Congress appointed George Washington to head the Continental army. Major battles were fought in such places as Boston, Massachusetts; Ticonderoga, New York; and Quebec. In November, the war reached Jefferson's Virginia when the royal governor, Lord Dunmore, placed the colony under martial law, established a base in the port town of Norfolk and began recruiting a Loyalist army. By a promise of freedom to those slaves who deserted their masters, he raised a black regiment. But in early December, a militia force of

Virginians and North Carolinians defeated Dunmore and forced him to flee Norfolk. On New Year's Day 1776, however, Dunmore returned with a British naval force and bombarded and burned the port. "They have destroyed one of the first towns in America," grieved a Virginian. "We are only sharing part of the sufferings of our American brethren, and can now glory in having received one of the keenest strokes of the enemy without flinching." He then concluded, Americans "must lay aside that childish fondness for Britain, and that foolish, tame dependence on her."

Only days later, Jefferson reached Virginia. As with most Americans, the Revolution was much on his mind. But fortunately for him, his country estate, Monticello, stood far removed from the coastal conflict and for a time he was able to relax with his family, engaging in such pleasures as tapping a large cask of aged Madeira wine, stocking his park with deer, and playing the violin accompanied by his wife on piano.

Yet even at Monticello, Jefferson could not avoid reflecting on the larger world. Early in February, Thomas Nelson, Jefferson's friend and fellow Virginia delegate to the Continental Congress, sent him a remarkable pamphlet with the simple title *Common Sense*. Published anonymously in January 1776, *Common Sense* circulated widely throughout the colonies. Its author, Thomas Paine, an Englishman who had settled in Philadelphia two years before, called on Americans to proclaim their independence immediately. In simple yet stirring language, Paine portrayed the colonists' struggle with Britain as a fight for human rights everywhere. "We have it in our power to begin the world over again, the birthday of a new world is at hand. . . . The cause of America is in great measure the cause of all mankind."

The main thrust of Paine's pamphlet was a scathing attack on monarchy (rule by a single hereditary leader, such as a king or queen). Despite the blood being shed, most Americans continued to believe that the king of England stood as their rightful ruler. In both the Old World and the New, people presumed monarchy essential, and for this reason the colonists had been reluctant to make a final break with Great Britain. At the time that Paine published *Common Sense*, there existed *no* successful republics—that is, governments without a monarch in which supreme power rested in the body of citizens entitled to vote. Paine extolled republicanism and ridiculed the whole notion of a hereditary monarch as an irrational and barbaric holdover from the Middle Ages (c. 500–1500, a period when Europe was primarily ruled by kings, queens, and princes).

Common Sense proved one of the most influential tracts ever printed. Within three months, it had sold more than 120,000 copies. In reference to Paine's publication, the *Connecticut Gazette* wrote: "Your production may justly be compared to a land-flood that sweeps all before it. We were blind, but on reading this enlightening work the scales have fallen from our eyes. . . . The doctrine of Independence hath been in times past, greatly disgustful; we abhorred the principle—it is now become our delightful theme, and commands our purest affections." Before Paine, monarchy was a respected, traditional institution; after *Common Sense,* more and more Americans, including Jefferson, became republicans willing to accept a full declaration of independence.

Soon after reading Paine's passionate pamphlet, Jefferson prepared to return to his duties in Philadelphia. But on March 31, 1776, his mother died unexpectedly from a stroke at the age of 57. Depressed and suffering from severe headaches, Jefferson delayed his departure until early May. He resumed his seat in Congress on May 14. The following day at a special convention in Williamsburg, Virginia declared itself independent, and as Jefferson later recalled, "the Convention of Virginia instructed their delegates in Congress to propose to that body to declare the colonies independent of Great Britain. . . ." Realizing that Virginia would need to draw up a new plan of government, Jefferson, in addition to his duties in Congress, devoted himself to drafting a constitution for the freshly launched commonwealth. As a preamble to this document, he also compiled a specific list of charges against Great Britain's King George III.

Although he seldom spoke in general congressional debate, Jefferson served effectively on many committees. Having written *A Summary View of the Rights of British America*, one of the most powerful pre–Revolutionary War pamphlets pleading the American cause (see chapter 2), he had a reputation as a lucid writer with a deep historical knowledge. Consequently, he was often called upon to draft reports. On June 7, 1776,

Jefferson, quietly sitting in his accustomed Windsor armchair in Philadelphia's State House, listened approvingly as fellow Virginian Richard Henry Lee moved "that the Congress should declare that these United colonies are, and of right ought to be free and independent states. . . ."

Debate on Lee's resolution revealed that whereas Virginia and New England supported independence, South Carolina, New York, Pennsylvania, and New Jersey were, in Jefferson's words, "not yet matured for falling from the parent stem, but that they were fast advancing to that state." Postponing the final decision on independence until July 1, Congress nevertheless agreed to appoint a committee to provide a declaration of independence. It consisted of John Adams of Massachusetts, the venerable Benjamin Franklin of Pennsylvania, Roger Sherman of Connecticut, Robert Livingston of New York, and Thomas Jefferson of Virginia.

Evidence suggests that the committee members met at Franklin's house to discuss the general form of the declaration. Adams later claimed that the others asked him and Jefferson to draft the document and that he insisted that Jefferson do it. "You are a Virginian," argued Adams, "and a Virginian ought to appear at the head of this business," and besides, he reasoned, "you can write ten times better than I can." So it came to pass that circumstances gave Jefferson, the youngest member of the committee, responsibility for writing the Declaration of Independence. Jefferson's genius would turn what otherwise might have been a routine political document into one of the most influential defenses of human rights ever written.

In the two weeks between June 13 and June 28, Jefferson labored on the declaration. Even as he wrote, the Revolution expanded as the British invaded Charleston, South Carolina. Busy with congressional matters during the days, he composed in the early morning and late into the evening, sitting in the airy second-floor parlor of the rooms he had recently rented on Market Street. Although he claimed not to have consulted any books, by 1776 Jefferson had been a serious student of history, law, and politics for many years. His knowledge ranged from the ancient Greek and Roman classics, which he read in the original, to contemporaries such as Paine. His aims, as he candidly stated were not to find out new principles, or new arguments, never before thought of, not merely to say things which had never been said before, but to place before mankind the common sense of the subject in terms so plain and firm as to command their assent, and to justify ourselves in the independent stand we are compelled to take. Neither aiming at originality of principle or sentiment, nor yet copied from any particular and previous writing, it was intended to be an expression of the American mind, and to give to that expression the proper tone and spirit called for by the occasion.

Actually Jefferson did draw directly on other writings, particularly his own. Working on a portable writing desk of his design, he spread out the charges against King George III that he had assembled for the Virginia constitution. These came to compose much of the longest section of the Declaration of Independence. Scholars have also suggested that George Mason's Virginia Declaration of Rights influenced Jefferson's famed philosophical paragraph. That Jefferson would be inspired by contemporary revolutionary writers is not surprising. But if some of the ideas expressed in the Declaration were borrowed, Jefferson's brilliance lay in his ability to express complex political and philosophical concepts in elegant, direct prose. He had, as John Adams noted, a "peculiar felicity of expression."

Completing a first draft, Jefferson submitted the document to Adams and Franklin, who advised only minor word changes. Incorporating these suggestions and making further revisions, Jefferson submitted what he considered a satisfactory text to the committee as a whole. The members unanimously approved his work and on June 28 delivered the Declaration to Congress where it was tabled pending action on Lee's resolution for independence.

Four days later, on July 2, after voting in favor of independence, Congress began debate on Jefferson's Declaration. For two and a half days, Congress, meeting as a committee of the whole, subjected every line and provision of the manifesto to close scrutiny. Jefferson suffered in silence as Congress slashed words and even whole paragraphs. From his perspective, the most glaring deletion was his condemnation of the slave trade. In Jefferson's draft, he had charged King George III as the instigator of this vile trade:

> He had waged cruel war against human nature itself, violating its most sacred rights of life and liberty in the persons of a distant people, who never offended him, captivating and carrying them into slavery in another hemisphere, or to incur miserable death in their transportation thither. This piratical warfare, the opprobrium of INFIDEL powers, is the warfare of the CHRISTIAN king of Great Britain. Determined to keep open a market where MEN should be bought and sold, he has prostituted his negative [veto] for suppressing every legislative attempt to prohibit or to restrain this execrable commerce. . . .

Jefferson later claimed that his efforts to end "enslaving the inhabitants of Africa was struck out in complaisance to South Carolina and Georgia. . . ." Yet Congress had more valid reasons for expunging this charge. It simply was not true that George III alone could be blamed for the slave trade when colonists from the North as well as the South had willingly participated in and profited from this reprehensible business for more than a century.

Nevertheless, Jefferson's intended message to the world was that slavery violated the universal right of human freedom. He indicted the king for infringing on the "sacred rights to life and liberty" of an African people. Unlike many of his time, he did not view blacks as belonging to a separate and unequal category. Just as with whites, he saw blacks as endowed by the Supreme Being with the sacred rights of life, liberty, and the pursuit of happiness. Clearly, therefore, the idea that Jefferson wrote the Declaration with whites only in mind is a myth.

The Virginian stewed as Congress cut and changed. To his dying day, he believed that his colleagues had weakened the document. Yet comparing his draft with the version that ultimately emerged, one would have to conclude that congressional changes and erasures strengthened the Declaration, contributing to greater directness and clarity of expression. Finally, on the evening of July 4, 1776, the delegates adopted the Declaration of Independence. Despite congressional tinkering, it remained very much the work of Thomas Jefferson.

On July 8, the sheriff of Philadelphia read the Declaration to a cheering throng gathered in the courtyard of the State House, later renamed Independence Hall. Following the reading, the crowd tore down the royal insignia before the State House, rang bells, and rejoiced well into the evening. Throughout the country, the Declaration fanned the flames of patriotism to passionate intensity. Americans fully committed themselves to revolution. "The people now are convinced of what we ought long since to have known," claimed a New Jersey reporter, "that our enemies have left us no middle way between perfect freedom and abject slavery."

On July 10, "loud huzzas [cheers], and the utmost demonstrations of joy," erupted as the Declaration was read at the head of each brigade of the Continental army posted in and around New York City, where only days before a vast British fleet had landed troops on nearby Staten Island. That evening, jubilant patriots tore down the huge mounted statue of King George III. American revolutionaries soon converted the two tons of lead of which the statue was made into musket balls so that, as one New Yorker put it, the king's men could feel the

John Trumbull's painting of the signing of the Declaration of Independence. At six feet two inches in height, Jefferson, holding the document, towers above Franklin to his right and Adams to his far left. (Yale University Art Gallery, Trumbull Collection)

Following a reading of the Declaration of Independence, an angry New York crowd tears down the statue of King George III. (The New York Public Library; Astor, Lenox and Tilden Foundations)

effect of "melted Majesty fired at them." Similar events erupted throughout the newly independent states as roused citizens rallied to the cause that Jefferson had done so much to ignite.

Yet it was several years before the authorship of the Declaration of Independence became generally known and its worldwide significance widely heralded. Jefferson in his later years basked in the fame the Declaration bestowed on him. Shortly before his death, he proudly instructed that his writing the Declaration be inscribed on his tombstone as the first of his accomplishments.

Like Paine's *Common Sense*, Jefferson's Declaration of Independence directed its charges against the king. With great brevity, Jefferson stated the indictment: "The history of the present King of Great Britain is a history of repeated injuries and usurpations, all having in direct object the establishment of an absolute tyranny over these states. To prove this, let facts be submitted to a candid world."

Jefferson then went on to offer proofs based on the historical experiences of the American people over the previous decade. He charged George III with such wrongdoings as refusing "his assent to laws, the most wholesome and necessary for the public good"; dissolving "Representative Houses repeatedly, for opposing with manly firmness his invasions on the rights of the people"; keeping "among us, in times of peace, standing armies without the consent of our legislatures"; combining "with others to subject us to a jurisdiction foreign to our constitution, and unacknowledged by our laws"; and plundering "our seas," ravaging "our coasts," burning "our towns," and destroying "the lives of our people."

Undoubtedly Jefferson realized that it was an oversimplification to blame all British actions offensive to the Americans on the king. Yet he had an explicit purpose in this. He clearly believed that the monarch stood as the last strong tie to the mother country. Parliamentary authority had already been repudiated repeatedly. The king was another matter. Many Americans persisted in viewing the monarch, at least symbolically, as the legitimate father of his subjects and as God's authority on earth. Creating a truly independent republic therefore necessitated the symbolic slaying of the king/father. Thomas Paine began this figurative patricide; Thomas Jefferson completed it.

As important as the accusations against George III were in securing widespread assent to independence, certainly the Declaration would be little remembered today were that all it contained. Unlike the wrathful tone of the passages assaulting the monarch, the beginning and closing sections of the Declaration are elegant and dignified. The document begins:

> When in the course of human events, it becomes necessary for one people to dissolve the political bands which have connected them with another, and to assume among the powers of the earth, the separate and equal station to which the laws of Nature and of Nature's God entitle them, a decent respect to the opinions of mankind requires that they should declare the causes which impel them to the separation.

This opening paragraph beautifully bestows an immediate sense of the solemn resolve of the Americans' cause and elevates the Revolution above colonial bickering to a struggle of universal significance "in the course of human events."

The stately concluding paragraph declares "That these United Colonies are, and of right ought to be, FREE AND

INDEPENDENT STATES. . . ." It ends with the ringing pledge: "And for the support of this Declaration, with a firm reliance on the protection of Divine Providence, we mutually pledge to each other our lives, our fortunes and our sacred honor."

More than any other part of the Declaration, however, it is the philosophical second paragraph that gives the document immortality:

> We hold these truths to be self-evident, that all men are created equal, that they are endowed by their Creator with certain unalienable rights, that among these are life, liberty and the pursuit of happiness. That to secure these rights, governments are instituted among men, deriving their just powers from the consent of the governed,—That whenever any form of government becomes destructive of these ends, it is the right of the people to alter or to abolish it, and to institute new government, laying its foundation on such principles and organizing its powers in such form, as to them shall seem most likely to effect their safety and happiness. Prudence, indeed, will dictate that governments long established should not be changed for light and transient causes; and accordingly all experience hath shown, that mankind are more disposed to suffer, while evils are sufferable, than to right themselves by abolishing the forms to which they are accustomed. But when a long train of abuses and usurpations, pursuing invariably the same object evinces a design to reduce them under absolute despotism, it is their right, it is their duty, to throw off such government, and to provide new guards for their future security.—Such has been the patient sufferance of these Colonies; and such is now the necessity which constrains them to alter their former systems of government. . . .

This remarkably compact and simple paragraph contains a complete philosophy of government—a revolutionary ideology that became the basic belief of the new nation.

Perhaps the most radical doctrine in the hierarchical world of the 18th century was the idea of *equality*: "all men are created equal." As a highly trained lawyer, Jefferson certainly meant that all men were equal before the law. Thus some 25 years later, on assuming the presidency in 1801, Jefferson's famed Inaugural Address called for "equal and exact justice to all men." Yet he also believed that people were equal because all originated from a single divine creation, possessed an innate moral sense, and had the same faculty of reason. Although individuals exhibited differing characteristics, they were equal on the basis of their common humanity. Additionally, he liked to contrast what he termed "the lovely equality" of Americans with the impoverished masses of Europe "loaded with misery by Kings, nobles, and priests." Throughout his long career, Jefferson did all he could to make land available to ordinary citizens. "Legislators," he insisted, "cannot invent too many devices for subdividing property. . . . Whenever there is in any country uncultivated lands and unemployed poor, it is clear that the laws of property have been so far extended as to violate natural rights." In subsequent generations, the Declaration's equality clause would become a rallying cry for workers, women, African Americans, gays, and other groups demanding their rights.

The second fundamental political doctrine of the Declaration was *natural rights*: "they are endowed by their Creator with certain unalienable rights, that among these are life, liberty and the pursuit of happiness." Such rights, it was assumed, belonged to human beings by their nature, not by the gift of society. Conjecture about natural rights was widespread among 18th-century intellectuals. The writings of Aristotle, Cicero, and other ancient authors stimulated such speculations. Even more direct an inspiration came from English philosopher John Locke's *Second Treatise on Government* (1689). Yet Locke's famed work cited "life, liberty, and property" as the basic natural rights. By substituting "pursuit of happiness" for "property," Jefferson's Declaration at once became more abstract and idealistic. It is not that Jefferson disapproved of property rights but rather that he saw property ownership as simply a means to achieving the higher goal of human happiness. Property, therefore, remained a civil and not a natural right. Thus the Declaration elevated human rights above mere property rights.

The third essential of the Declaration's political philosophy was the radical principle of the *sovereignty of the people*: "governments are instituted among men, deriving their just powers from the consent of the governed." Whereas in virtually all past societies rulers subordinated the rights of the people, Jefferson's

Declaration made the people the ultimate authority. The Declaration thus launched America as a unique experiment in democracy.

The capstone of the Declaration's political philosophy was the *right of revolution*: "That whenever any form of government becomes destructive of these ends, it is the right of the people to alter or to abolish it, and to institute new government." Since government rested on the sovereignty of the people, should that government become tyrannical and infringe on the natural rights of its citizens then the people were justified in overthrowing it. Recourse to revolution, Jefferson insisted, should not be undertaken at the least provocation, but only after "a long train of abuses and usurpations." Despite this note of forbearance, the right of revolution proved a provocative principle that legitimized radical democratic forces first in America and ultimately throughout much of the world.

The Declaration of Independence took the squabble between the colonies and Great Britain and elevated the American Revolution to a universal struggle for human rights and democracy. The document gave Americans a political philosophy that the Revolutionary generation would soon set about institutionalizing in the new nation. Beginning with the outbreak of the French Revolution in 1789, the Declaration would help usher in an age of revolution that still influences the course of history. "The flames kindled on the 4th of July, 1776," boasted Jefferson nearly half a century later, "have spread over too much of the globe to be extinguished by the feeble engines of despotism; on the contrary, they will consume these engines and all who work them." Indeed what Abraham Lincoln declared on the eve of America's Civil War still rings true: "All honor to Jefferson—to the man who, in the concrete pressure of a struggle for national independence . . . had the coolness, forecast, and capacity to introduce into a merely revolutionary document, an abstract truth, applicable to all men and all times, and so to embalm it there, that to-day, and in coming days, it shall be a rebuke and a stumbling-block to the very harbingers of reappearing tyranny and oppression." The Declaration of Independence remains Thomas Jefferson's most majestic political and literary monument.

2

THE MAKING OF A REVOLUTIONARY

Thomas Jefferson was born April 13, 1743, on an estate called Shadwell in what is now Albemarle County, Virginia. At the time of his birth, Shadwell lay on the fringe of western settlement in the English colony of Virginia. Situated on the rolling hills of the Piedmont to the west of the fertile plains of the Tidewater, Shadwell's simple frame house overlooked the Rivanna River, a branch of the James. Through a gap to the southwest could be seen the distant Blue Ridge, the first range of the Appalachians.

Shadwell's proprietor, Peter Jefferson, Thomas's father, though self-educated, had become a large landholder, slave owner, and tobacco planter, as well as a surveyor, map maker, and political leader. He instilled in his son a love of nature and Indian lore. He also stressed the importance of hard work and physical exercise, and, denied the opportunity to receive a formal education himself, he insisted that his son be given a thorough classical training. Although Thomas was only 14 when his father died, Peter Jefferson had a profound and lasting influence on his son. He also left him a wealthy young man by the standards of the day. His will bequeathed to his eldest son the Shadwell house, nearly 5,000 acres, some 26 slaves, and various horses, cattle, sheep, and hogs.

Thomas Jefferson's mother, Jane Randolph, came from one of the wealthiest and most distinguished Tidewater families who, Jefferson later noted in his *Autobiography*, "trace their pedigree far back in England and Scotland, to which let every man ascribe the faith and merit he chooses." Despite poking fun at his mother's aristocratic lineage, being related to the Randolphs assured Jefferson's social position among the first families of colonial Virginia.

Thomas Jefferson's earliest memory was of leaving Shadwell, when he was about two. A slave on horseback carried him some 70 miles over wilderness trails and rough roads to Tuckahoe, the large Tidewater estate of the late William Randolph. In his will, Randolph, Jane Randolph's first cousin, had asked that his friend Peter Jefferson look after his children and property on his death. At Tuckahoe young Thomas was part of a large extended family on a grand plantation with many slaves. Here he got his first schooling from a private tutor who taught Jefferson, his four sisters, and the three Randolph children.

In 1752, when Jefferson was nine, the family returned to Shadwell. Soon after he was sent to study Greek, Latin, and French at the school of the Reverend William Douglas, a Scottish clergyman. He boarded with the Reverend Douglas, but traveled the 12 miles to Shadwell to spend weekends and vacations. While at home, Jefferson loved riding in the forest; swimming, canoeing, and fishing in the Rivanna; and meandering about the countryside often in company with his favorite sister Jane, three years his senior. An able student and avid reader, Jefferson also took delight in his father's volumes of William Shakespeare, Johnathan Swift, and Joseph Addison. During these years, he learned to play the violin, an instrument that he would enjoy throughout his life. He would later proclaim music "the favorite passion of my soul."

After the death of his father, Jefferson went to study with the Reverend James Maury, whom he later characterized as "a correct classical scholar." Jefferson's early mastery of Latin and Greek opened up to him a rich storehouse of history, literature, drama, poetry, philosophy, and political theory. He would remain an ardent student of the classics for the remainder of his days.

In the spring of 1760, Jefferson left his beloved hills of Shadwell to attend the College of William and Mary, located in Williamsburg, Virginia's capital. Already more than six feet tall with tousled reddish hair and a freckled, ruddy face, the lanky young man was bright and eager, yet somewhat shy, awkward, and unpolished. William and Mary in Jefferson's day was not a distinguished institution. Its fewer than 100 students were largely taught by a few ill-trained Anglican clergymen. There was, however, one exemplary exception. "It was my great good fortune, and what probably fixed the destinies of my life," Jefferson later maintained

> that Dr. William Small of Scotland was then Professor of Mathematics, a man profound in most of the useful branches of science, with a happy talent of communication, correct and gentlemanly manners, and an enlarged and liberal mind. He, most happily for me, became soon attached to me, and made me his daily companion when not engaged in the school; and from his conversation I got my first views of the expansion of science and the system of things in which we are placed.

In addition to being a superb mathematics teacher, Small also lectured on ethics, philosophy, rhetoric, and literature. Small further broadened Jefferson's educational horizons by introducing him to two other wise gentlemen—George Wythe and Governor Francis Fauquier. Wythe, a classics scholar and Virginia's most respected lawyer, would become Jefferson's lifelong mentor and friend. Governor Fauquier, a courtly, learned Londoner, was in Jefferson's estimation the "ablest man" ever to serve as Virginia's royal governor. Fauquier loved good food, wine, music, and conversation, and soon welcomed Jefferson as a weekly guest at dinner parties held in the Governor's Palace. Here in the company of the governor, Small, and Wythe, Jefferson claimed to have "heard more good sense, more rational and philosophical conversations, than in all my life besides."

Through such men along with his voracious reading, Jefferson became swept up by the enlightened thought of the age—an intellectual ferment that percolated through learned society in Europe and the colonies. Beginning with the great scientific discoveries of the 17th century that culminated in the work of Isaac Newton, enlightened thinkers came to believe that the universe was governed by natural laws. Just as Newton's law of gravitation seemed to explain not only the falling of an apple but even the movement of the planets, 18th-century intellectuals assumed that similar universal laws also applied to the social and moral realms.

Reason and sense experience were deemed the only valid sources of knowledge. Enlightened intellectuals assumed that the world could be made a better place if only social institutions could be based on reason and nature's laws, and not on traditions and superstitions. Rejecting the Christian concept of original sin, such thinkers explained evil as the result of bad institutions that were not rationally conceived. This optimistic philosophy would lay the intellectual groundwork for both the American and French Revolutions and the whole rise of modern democracy.

Fascinated by the enlightened world view, Jefferson devoted himself diligently to his studies, sometimes reading as many as 15 hours a day. In today's complex world, scholars tend to specialize. But in the 18th century, the goal of the educated gentleman was to master all fields. For many individuals this resulted in little more than a nodding acquaintance with a variety of subjects. Jefferson, on the other hand, with his

Williamsburg's Main Street as viewed from the college windows (*Scribner's Monthly*, November 1875)

Williamsburg's Raleigh Tavern served as a frequent gathering place for both social and political activities (Scribner's Monthly, November 1875)

insatiable appetite for learning and extraordinary intellectual abilities explored many topics in depth. The advice he offered to a friend gives a good idea of his study habits. He advocated rising early and "till eight o'clock in the morning" reading agriculture, chemistry, anatomy, zoology, botany, ethics, and religion. "From eight to twelve read law. . . . From twelve to one read politics. . . . In the afternoon read history. . . . From dark to bedtime: belles lettres, criticism, rhetoric. . . . Read the best of the poets . . . but among these Shakespeare must be singled out by one who wishes to learn the full powers of the English language." Physical exercise also had its place in Jefferson's regime. He often rode his horse, ran a mile or more daily, and loved taking long country walks.

But Jefferson did much more than study and exercise while living in Williamsburg. Though a provincial town of fewer than 1,000 residents, Williamsburg was by far the largest community Jefferson had ever seen. As the capital and the location of Virginia's only college, Williamsburg was the colony's political and cultural center. When the House of Burgesses (the colonial legislature) was in session, the planter elite gathered there and many maintained townhouses in the capital. Sons of wealthy planters were Jefferson's classmates. His closest friend, John Page, for instance, lived at Roswell, the largest plantation house in Virginia. There were lavish parties and dances at the elegant Raleigh Tavern. Touring London actors performed the plays of Shakespeare and others. Horse races, cock fights, cards, dice, and sundry amusements attracted students and planters alike. Jefferson resisted most temptations. He never used tobacco, played cards, bet on the horses, or fought. He liked good wine, but generally refused stronger drink. Yet though he was more studious and serious than his fellow classmates, he loved dancing, music, and flirting with pretty girls.

Among the young ladies that Jefferson met, he was particularly smitten by Rebecca Burwell, the attractive 16-year-old sister of a college classmate. For a time, he could think of no one else and yet was too shy to confess his love to Rebecca. "How does R. B. do?" he wrote to his friend Page from Shadwell. "Had I better stay here and do nothing, or go down and do less? . . . Inclination tells me to go, receive my sentence, and be no longer in suspense; but reason says, if you go, and your attempt proves unsuccessful, you will be ten times more wretched than ever." Finally at a dance, Jefferson managed to blurt out a half-hearted marriage proposal, asking Rebecca to wait for him while he went abroad for a few years. Not surprisingly, the young lady soon announced her engagement to another. "Well the Lord bless her," the unsuccessful suitor exclaimed. "Many

William and Mary College (*Scribner's Monthy*, November 1875)

and great are the comforts of a single state."

By the time Jefferson graduated from college in the spring of 1762, he possessed a far greater breadth of learning than most of his contemporaries. But what was he to do with his life? Although a large landowner, settling down to a life of tobacco planting held little appeal. Other professions available to Virginia gentlemen—the ministry or the military—he also disdained. Only law appeared as a calling that could both challenge him intellectually and serve society. In Williamsburg, Jefferson knew several lawyers whom he admired. There was his relative Peyton Randolph, a most respected lawyer who had been educated at London's Inner Temple; his slightly older friend Patrick Henry who was making a name for himself as a fiery courtroom orator; and above all there was George Wythe who agreed to take Jefferson on as his law student.

At the time, there were no law schools. To become a lawyer, one read and worked as an apprentice of an already established lawyer. Wythe, about 35 when Jefferson commenced studying with him, proved a perfect choice. Like Jefferson, he was a classics scholar with a broad humanistic education. Thoroughly versed in Roman and English law, he taught law as an Enlightenment science. In addition to training Jefferson, Wythe would later teach such notables as Chief Justice John Marshall and Henry Clay. But Jefferson remained his favorite pupil and to him he willed his fine library. For his part, Jefferson described Wythe as "my faithful and beloved mentor in youth and my most affectionate friend through life."

Unlike Patrick Henry who had started practicing the law after a mere six weeks of lackadaisical reading, Jefferson spent five years in extensive study. Under Wythe's skillful guidance, he plowed through numerous weighty law books from the 17th-century English jurist Sir Edward Coke to the enlightened French contemporary Baron de Montesquieu. He studied actual written laws from ancient times to the present, reading them whenever possible in the original, even mastering Anglo-Saxon to understand the origins of common law, the English system of judicial precedents that had developed over centuries based on court decisions and custom. As had been his habit for some time, Jefferson wrote extensive notes on his readings in a *Commonplace Book*. Finally in 1767 the 24-year-old Jefferson was admitted to the bar.

He quickly became a successful practicing attorney, though he never attained the notoriety of his friend Patrick Henry. "Mr. Jefferson," a contemporary noted, "drew copiously from the depths of the law, Mr. Henry from the recesses of the human heart." Although thoroughly versed in English common law, the enlightened Jefferson, in an effort to free a slave in 1770, referred to a higher "law of nature." "Under the law of nature," he argued, "all men are born free, every one comes into the world with a right to his own person, which includes the liberty of moving and using it at his own will." Jefferson lost this case, but would soon find that reference to the law of nature could be deployed in the growing rift between the colonies and Great Britain.

Tensions with Britain had first shown themselves in the aftermath of the successful French and Indian War that drove France from the North American continent. When that war ended in 1763, Britain looked to the colonies to help raise revenue to fill its depleted treasury. In 1765, Parliament passed the Stamp Act, a law requiring the colonists to purchase stamps to be placed on all publications and legal documents. This was the first time that the British Parliament had ever levied an internal tax on the colonies. Violent outcries occurred throughout the colonies. Thomas Jefferson, still a law student, stood listening in the doorway of the House of Burgesses on May 30, 1765, when he heard his friend Patrick Henry declare that the "sole right and power to levy taxes and impositions upon the inhabitants of this colony" rests with the colonials' elected representatives. Henry went on to denounce King George III, leading some of the more conservative members to mutter "treason." But to Jefferson, the fiery young lawyer's speech rang true."

Opposition to the Stamp Act escalated throughout the colonies and ultimately forced Parliament to repeal this hated tax. However, in 1766 Parliament passed the Declaratory Act, asserting the right to legislate for the colonies, and made good on that threat the following year, passing the Townshend Act. Since the colonies had balked at an internal tax, this new legislation imposed an external tax, a duty on various goods the colonies imported. Colonial protests over these Townshend duties was still raging in May 1769, when Jefferson took the oath of office as an elected member of the House of Burgesses. He had just turned 26.

Jefferson's political career began auspiciously. He joined in passing a unanimous resolution declaring that only the House of Burgesses had the right to levy taxes on the colony of Virginia. In retaliation, the royal governor, Baron Botetourt, dissolved the House, but most of the burgesses simply reconvened and continued their business in the Raleigh Tavern's elegant Apollo Room where Jefferson had once made his ill-fated proposal to Rebecca Burwell. There, with Jefferson's enthusiastic support, they agreed to boycott British goods until the Townshend duties were repealed. Other colonies also adopted nonimportation agreements, and the business of British exporters drastically declined. This economic coercion soon succeeded, and in 1770 Parliament repealed all duties, except for a tax on tea. Despite the remaining tea tax, left as a badge of Parliament's claimed authority, American resistance collapsed and, for the moment, the business of the burgesses returned to routine affairs.

During this period while Jefferson divided his time between his legislative duties and his law practice, he also undertook the building of a new house. In his boyhood rambles, he had been repeatedly attracted to a hilltop across the Rivanna from the Shadwell house. Often while home from his college and law studies in Williamsburg, he would paddle across the river, climb the hill, gaze out at the far vistas, and dream someday of building a house there. After he taught himself Italian, he came to call his hill "Monticello," meaning small mountain. In the late 1760s, the building of Monticello began. It would become Jefferson's avocation for nearly a lifetime (see chapter 8).

In February 1770, a fire destroyed the Shadwell house, including Jefferson's papers and extensive library. The blaze spurred him to speed work on the new house, and by November a small brick cottage, a tiny part of the grand design, stood ready for occupancy. By February 1771, Jefferson boasted in a letter: "I have lately removed to the mountain from whence this is dated. I have here but one room, which, like the cobbler's serves me for parlour for kitchen and hall. I may add, for bed chamber and study too."

It was to this small house that Jefferson would bring his bride in the midst of a January 1772 blizzard. Jefferson met Martha Wayles Skelton, an attractive young widow, in the fall of 1770. Martha was the daughter of John Wayles, a wealthy lawyer and planter with a large estate called Forest not too far from Williamsburg. Jefferson soon fell in love for the first time since his adolescent flirtation with Rebecca. By August 1771 he confided that "in every scheme of happiness she is placed in the fore-ground, as the principal figure. Take that away, and it is no picture for me." On New Year's Day 1772, they were married at Forest and later that month set out for Monticello in what Jefferson claimed was "the deepest snow we have ever seen." The young couple settled in happily and in September their first child, Martha (nicknamed Patsy), was born. Jefferson loved domestic life at Monticello, but momentous events would soon draw him away from his idyllic mountain.

The husband and new father missed the legislative session of 1772, though as Jefferson noted "nothing of particular excitement" occurred. But when the House of Burgesses met in March 1773, he was present and helped establish an intercolonial system of committees of correspondence so that the separate colonies could be kept informed of what each was doing in the ongoing conflict with Great Britain. Annoyed at this, the royal governor terminated the legislative session after only 11 days and did not call the burgesses back until May 1774.

Soon after, Jefferson's personal life was greatly affected by the death of his best friend and brother-in-law, Dabney Carr, and the death of his father-in-law, John Wayles. Carr had attended Maury's school with Jefferson and in 1765 had married his sister Martha. Jefferson loved him dearly and had him buried at Monticello. Several years later, after Jefferson's house had expanded in size, Martha Carr and her children would come to live at Monticello. Less than two weeks after Carr's passing, John Wayles died. The Jeffersons inherited a vast estate, 135 slaves, and a large debt.

By the time the burgesses met in May 1774, the long simmering crisis with Britain was again coming to a boil. In retaliation for Bostonians dumping the East India Company's tea into the water, Great Britain closed Boston Harbor to all commerce effective June 1, 1774. As an expression of solidarity with Boston, Jefferson suggested that the House of Burgesses declare June 1 a day of fasting and prayer "to turn the hearts of the King and Parliament to moderation and justice."

Once more the enraged royal governor dismissed the burgesses, but this time the representatives quickly reconvened in the Raleigh Tavern and agreed that "an attack on any one colony should be considered as an attack on the whole." They also proposed that the colonies meet in a general congress to discuss their common problems. Before departing Williamsburg, they pledged to hold a convention on August 1 to choose delegates to attend the First Continental Congress.

Back at Monticello, Jefferson busied himself drawing up resolutions and proposals in preparation for the August meeting. Illness, however, forced him to miss the convention, but he sent on the paper he had intended to deliver. This was printed under the title *A Summary View of the Rights of British America* and soon reprinted elsewhere in the colonies and London. The author was listed only as "A Native, and Member of the House of Burgesses," but knowledge of Jefferson's authorship rapidly spread and with it his reputation as a lucid writer and a great advocate of American rights. Jefferson emerged as a major national and international voice in the vanguard of the Revolutionary movement.

By the summer of 1774, imperial relations had deteriorated to the point of becoming "intolerable" to Jefferson and many other Americans. But public sentiment did not yet favor independence from Britain. Jefferson's *Summary View* boldly set forth the rights of Americans and enumerated a list of specific grievances against both Parliament and the crown that proved "a deliberate, systematical plan of reducing us to slavery." He claimed that

> our emigration from England to this country gave her no more rights over us, than the emigrations of the Danes and Saxons gave to the present authorities of the mother country over England. . . . Our ancestors, before their emigration to America, were the free inhabitants of the British dominions in Europe, and possessed a right, which nature has given to all men, of departing from the country in which chance, not choice has placed them, of going in quest of new habitations, and of there establishing new societies, under such laws and regulations as to them shall seem most likely to promote public happiness.

The logic of Jefferson's argument pointed to independence: Americans possessed the natural right to govern themselves. But he stopped short of this and recognized allegiance to a common king as the only remaining bond of empire. Although even the monarch, as Jefferson saw it, was "no more than the chief officer of the people, appointed by the laws, and circumscribed with definite powers . . . and consequently subject to their superintendance." Should the king violate this social contract, the people could wield "sacred and sovereign rights of punishment, reserved in the hands of the people for cases of extreme necessity."

Although Jefferson did not attend the First Continental Congress, which met from September 5 to October 26, 1774, his *Summary View* was much discussed, even though most delegates found it too radical. Yet the pamphlet continued to circulate widely, and over time, as imperial relations worsened, its logic became more compelling. By June 1775, when Jefferson joined the Virginia delegation for the Second Continental Congress at Philadelphia, fighting had already begun. Three days after Jefferson's arrival, his friend and fellow Virginia delegate George Washington left Philadelphia for Boston as the newly elected commander of the Continental army.

Jefferson, though only 32, brought with him to Philadelphia, according to John Adams, "a reputation for literature, science, and a happy talent for composition." He was quickly picked to join Adams, Benjamin Franklin, and Richard Henry Lee in drafting a stinging reply to Great Britain's latest "conciliatory proposition." Shortly thereafter, he and John Dickinson of Pennsylvania composed the important Declaration of the Causes and Necessity of Taking Up Arms. Less than a year later, Jefferson's recognized talents earned him appointment to the committee selected to draw up the Declaration of Independence.

3

REFORMING VIRGINIA

Once Congress adopted the Declaration of Independence, assuring that the new nation would be based on sound republican principles, Thomas Jefferson looked forward to retiring from the national scene and returning to Virginia. Worried about his wife's poor health, he requested that the Virginia House of Delegates (successor to the House of Burgesses) appoint someone else to take his place in the Continental Congress. Finally in early September 1776, his wish was granted, and he quickly rode home to Monticello.

Jefferson's concern for his wife was certainly sincere. But there were other reasons as well why he willingly gave up his seat in Congress to return to Virginia. Although a plan of confederation was before Congress, Jefferson, along with most other Revolutionary leaders, assumed that real political sovereignty would continue to reside in the individual states. He wished to participate in republicanizing Virginia. The Revolution to him meant much more that gaining independence from Great Britain. It was an opportunity to start over, to create governments and laws based on reason. Jefferson was bent on seizing the opportunity for reform while the Revolutionary spirit still burned: "The time for fixing every essential right on a legal basis is while our rulers are honest, and ourselves united. From the conclusion of this war we shall be going down hill."

Elected to the Virginia House of Delegates, Jefferson took his seat in October 1776 and soon began his far-reaching efforts to create a republican utopia. His major goals included devising easier access to land ownership; establishing religious freedom; providing free public education; streamlining and liberalizing Virginia's penal code; and ending the slave trade and eventually abolishing slavery. Through such measures he hoped that "every fiber would be eradicated of ancient or feudal aristocracy; and a foundation laid for government truly republican."

More conservative delegates frequently balked at Jefferson's sweeping recommendations. His educational reforms were a case in point. To Jefferson and many other Revolutionary leaders, education was the cornerstone of republican government. Since a republic rested on the will of the people, it would not long survive unless the people were adequately informed and virtuous. In 1778, in the midst of the Revolution, Jefferson brought before the Virginia legislature the Bill for the More General Diffusion of Knowledge. He proposed a three-tiered educational system with elementary schools, grammar schools, and a university topping the pyramid. While all children would attend the elementary schools, only the most qualified young men would advance to the grammar school level, and from these the highest achievers would be sent on to university. Such a system, Jefferson believed, was well adapted to the circumstances and abilities of all students. It aimed first of all "to illuminate, as far as practicable, the minds of the people at large," and second to guarantee "that those persons, whom nature hath endowed with genius and virtue, should be rendered by liberal education worthy to receive, and able to guard the sacred deposit of the rights and liberties of their fellow citizens and that they should be called to that charge without regard to wealth, birth or other accidental condition or circumstance."

Jefferson's program was the first educational proposal that envisioned public support from the lowest elementary levels to the university at the apex, and it was also the first plan to place merit above money by making talent the sole criterion of promotion. Even the notion that the children of the rich and the poor should be educated in common was a radical departure from standard practice.

Unfortunately, Jefferson's educational design failed to pass the Virginia legislature. Not until 1796 was a school bill enacted and this provided for elementary schools only and left to the county courts the power to put it into operation. Most county courts failed to do this and, to Jefferson's dismay, the state remained without a true system of public education.

Jefferson's efforts to end slavery met with a similar fate, although he did succeed in banning the further import of slaves into Virginia (see chapter 9). His proposal to fund a state library also fell on deaf ears. Despite these and other failures or only partial successes, no single individual in Virginia or any other state drafted more bills that were adopted during the years of the Revolution.

Jefferson ranked among his major achievements the abolition of entail and primogeniture—two tokens of feudalism, the social and economic system in Europe during the Middle Ages in which ordinary citizens worked on lands owned by a landed aristocracy. By the law of entail, estates could not be divided, even generations after the original owner's death. By the law of primogeniture, when a person died without having written a will, all that individual's property passed to the eldest son. The purpose of these laws was to perpetuate a landed aristocracy and Jefferson deemed their repeal "essential to a well ordered republic." He succeeded in his fight against entail and primogeniture, effectively ending the last vestiges of feudalism. To John Adams he later boasted that the abolishment of entails and primogeniture "laid the axe to the root of Pseudo-aristocracy [the landed gentry]."

Another major victory for Jefferson was the passage of his Statute for Religious Freedom. To him, church and state should be completely separate: "The legitimate powers of government extend to such acts only as are injurious to others. But it does me no injury for my neighbor to say there are twenty gods, or no God. It neither picks my pocket nor breaks my leg. . . . Reason and free inquiry are the only effectual agents against error."

In colonial Virginia, the Anglican Church enjoyed tax support and special legal status. Over the years, however, many Presbyterians, Methodists, Baptists, and other non-Anglicans had settled and resented having to pay taxes to support the Anglican clergy. As Jefferson saw it, to require people to contribute money to maintain *any* church was to deprive them of freedom. European nations had a long history of religious strife. If America was to develop peacefully as a multiethnic country, then religious freedom was essential. Jefferson's statute provided for a complete separation of church and state and helped make that doctrine basic to the new nation.

During this period, the delegates chose Jefferson to head a committee to revise, amend, or repeal the laws of Virginia and report back their recommendations to the House. This comprehensive revision proved a major undertaking and occupied Jefferson and his friend George Wythe for over two years. Virginia had inherited a long tradition of English common law going back even before the Magna Carta, the "great charter" of English liberties, forced from King John by the English barons in 1215. To these the Virginia legislature had added numerous new laws over more than a century and a half. Many of these laws were harsh. Witches and heretics, for instance, could still be burned at the stake; stealing a horse warranted the death penalty; whipping and even maiming remained legal punishments.

The very language of the old laws also presented a problem. As Jefferson noted, many of the statutes were verbose, "their endless tautologies [repetitions], their involution of case within case, and parentheses within parenthesis" rendered them perplexing and incomprehensible, "not only to common readers, but to the lawyers themselves."

Working slowly and meticulously, Jefferson and Wythe went through every law, striking out some, and modifying others to eliminate barbaric punishments and muddled English. When they finished this process of codification, they had reduced the long list of English and colonial laws to 126 lucid, brief bills that filled only 90 printed pages. The final report revised the criminal code to make it more humane and enlightened. The new code restricted the death penalty to murder and treason. Hard labor was substituted for whipping or other physical punishment. Laws enforcing religious beliefs were abolished. Contrary to common law practice, Jefferson authored a new law to make it easy for immigrants to become citizens.

In June 1779, Jefferson's committee submitted their document to the Assembly. But rather than voting on the report as a whole, the delegates chose to take up each of the 126 bills separately. Politics took over. Conservatives delayed many of the bills and defeated others. However, by the mid-1780s, championed by Jefferson's young friend James Madison, the greater part of the 126 bills had been enacted. To a remarkable degree, Jefferson had succeeded in transforming Virginia into a modern, humane republic.

That same June 1779 in which Jefferson presented the revised laws to the Assembly, that body elected him governor of Virginia. He was 36 and the recognized leader of the republican forces. Yet the tactful temperament and philosophical nature that had brought him great success as a legislator would prove less useful for a wartime governor. Jefferson would later confess to being "unprepared by his line of life and education for the command of armies." He inherited a difficult situation. From the outset of the Revolution, Virginia had generously sent troops and supplies to Washington's army fighting in the North. But six months after Jefferson took office, the British, unable to defeat Washington there, shifted their major military effort to the South. A large British army under the command of Lord Cornwallis invaded the Carolinas. Fearing an attack on Williamsburg by sea, the Assembly voted to move the capital further inland to the village of Richmond.

By the spring of 1780, the success of the Revolution appeared in doubt. Jefferson had been doing all he could to aid the war effort in the Carolinas, sending the state's militia and what weapons and stores could be scraped together. But he operated under increasing obstacles—inflation; lack of arms, supplies, and fighting men; declining morale and outright disloyalty; and Indian attacks on the frontier.

Then on May 12, Charleston fell to the British and most of the Virginia forces were captured. Cornwallis's troops began moving northward. Virginia lay open to invasion. Governor Jefferson urgently appealed to Congress for men and arms. To General Washington he confided: "We are endeavouring to collect as large a body to oppose [the British] as we can arm. This will be lamentably inadequate if the Enemy be in any force; it is Mortifying to suppose it possible that a people able and zealous to contend with their Enemy should be reduced to fold their Arms for want of the means of defence; yet no resources that we know of, ensure us against this event."

In late December 1780, a British fleet bearing the troops of General Benedict Arnold entered Chesapeake Bay. Arnold's appearance particularly galled Virginians, as only weeks before this once heroic American general had turned traitor and defected to the British. Early in January 1781, the fleet sailed up the James River and landed Arnold's army for an attack on Richmond. Jefferson tried to muster the militia to defend the capital, but to no avail. Arnold's troops marched into the town and put Jefferson and the rest of the government to flight. They burned some buildings and destroyed a nearby foundry before withdrawing. Jefferson had done all he could to avert this humiliation, and, in fact, the damage Arnold inflicted proved minor. Nevertheless, many Virginians held the governor personally responsible for this dishonor.

That spring General Cornwallis, having suffered defeat in North Carolina, turned in desperation northward and marched his army into Virginia. Belatedly, Washington dispatched a 900-man force of Continentals under the leadership of a major general, the marquis de Lafayette, a French nobleman who had joined the American cause and distinguished himself as a valiant soldier. But badly outnumbered, Lafayette's troops could do little to stop the British onslaught, and once again Richmond fell to the enemy. In late May, the government took refuge in Charlottesville, not far from Monticello. Jefferson's second term as governor was to expire on June 2, and he had already informed the Assembly that he would not accept a third term. But before a vote could be taken to elect a new governor, the arrival of a British raiding party once more put the government to flight. Only the heroic all-night ride of Captain Jack Jouett of the Virginia militia warned the legislators in time to get away. Jouett continued on to Monticello, reaching Jefferson just ahead of the redcoats. The governor and his family barely escaped.

Again suffering humiliation, the Assembly on June 12, 1781, adopted a resolution calling for an investigation of the conduct of the governor. Of particular concern was "the total want of opposition to Arnold" during his sacking of Richmond. But by the time the inquiry was to be held in December, the Revolution had been won. With the aid of French troops and the French fleet, the army of General Washington had finally forced Cornwallis to surrender at Yorktown. Jefferson appeared before the Assembly, read the charges and answered them. Satisfied, the

Assembly unanimously passed a resolution of commendation and thanks, explaining that "popular rumours, gaining some degree of credence, by more pointed Accusations, rendered it necessary to make an enquiry into his conduct, and delayed that retribution of public gratitude, so eminently merited."

Despite this apology, Jefferson remained embittered and vowed to retire from public life. He even turned down an offer from the Continental Congress to join Franklin and Adams as one of the peace commissioners to negotiate with the British in Paris. "Were it possible for me to determine again to enter into public business there is no appointment whatever which would have been so agreeable to me," he wrote. "But I have taken my final leave of every thing of that nature, have retired to my farm, my family and books from which I think nothing will ever more separate me."

Back at his beloved Monticello, Jefferson took advantage of his leisure to organize and write an informative treatise on the state of Virginia. This was in response to a series of queries he had received from François Barbé-Marbois, secretary to the French delegation at Philadelphia. The questions concerned geography, natural resources, population, government, laws, religion, education, commerce and manufactures, and various other matters. Jefferson had long been collecting information on Virginia in his notebooks. Now Marbois's queries gave him the opportunity to organize this material in a coherent presentation. The result would be *Notes on the State of Virginia*, the only book that Jefferson ever authored. Published in France in 1785, *Notes* went through many editions and enhanced Jefferson's reputation as a scientist and preeminent Enlightenment thinker. Today the book is admired as the most significant scientific and political treatise of the Revolutionary era and as a pioneer work in terms of the American literature of travel and exploration.

Jefferson's book ranges widely. Although largely focused on Virginia, his commentary discusses such general topics as the proper organization of republican government, religious freedom, education, the moral superiority of farming as an occupation, Native Americans, and the problem of slavery. Throughout, the book reveals Jefferson's acute interest in natural history and provides accurate descriptions of birds, animals, trees, and plants. As a scientist, he reported his own precise observations, and where possible verified these by reference to the studies of others.

One aim of Jefferson was to refute the theory of the French naturalist Comte de Buffon that aborigines and animals of the New World were smaller and less fit than in Europe. Jefferson lavished praise on Native Americans and argued that "we shall probably find that they are formed in mind as well as in body, on the same module [standard] with the 'Homo sapiens Europaeus.'" He and others he enlisted in his project measured and weighed various animals to statistically disprove Buffon. An American elk, for instance, weighed 300 pounds more than its puny European cousin. Later, when in France, Jefferson, at great expense, had the horns, hide, and skeleton of a huge moose shipped from New Hampshire so that he might show it to Buffon. Seeing this, the renown French scientist apologized: "I should have consulted you, Mr. Jefferson, before I wrote my *Natural History*."

Jefferson clearly enjoyed retired life, and his mountaintop home, Monticello, now vastly expanded, was already a place of legend. Visiting there in the spring of 1782, the Chevalier de Chastellux, a general in the French army and friend of Lafayette's, was captivated by Jefferson and his house. He described his host as "a man, not yet forty, tall, and with a mild and pleasing countenance, but whose mind and attainments could serve in lieu of all outward graces; an American, who, without ever having quitted his own country, is Musician, Draftsman, Surveyor, Astronomer, Natural Philosopher, Jurist, and Statesman . . . and finally a Philosopher. . . . It seemed as if from his youth he had placed his mind, as he had done his house, on an elevated situation, from which he might contemplate the universe."

Chastellux envied Jefferson's domestic happiness: He had "a gentle and amiable wife, some pretty children he brings up with great care, a house to beautify and great possessions to improve, science and art to cultivate; this is what is left of Mr. Jefferson, after having played a distinguished role on the theatre of the New World."

Sadly, this domestic bliss was not to last. On May 8, 1782, only days after Chastellux left, Martha Jefferson gave birth to another girl, Lucy Elizabeth. This was the sixth child to be born in 10 years. Three children had died in infancy and each pregnancy and birth had been difficult. On May 20, Jefferson wrote to his friend James Monroe that "Mrs. Jefferson had added another daughter to our family. She has been ever since and still continues very dangerously ill." She would never recover. Jefferson stayed by her bedside and nursed her through the summer. On September 6, she died.

Heartbroken, Jefferson fainted and remained unconscious for so long that his sister Martha Carr feared he would never come to. When he did revive, he shut himself in his library for three weeks. Still despondent after this, his daughter, Patsy recalled that "he was incessantly on horseback, rambling about the mountain, in the least frequented roads, and just as often through the woods." To Chastellux he confessed that before his wife's death, "my scheme of life had been determined. I had folded myself in the arms of retirement, and rested all prospect of future happiness on domestic and literary objects. A single event wiped away all my plans and left me a blank which I had not the spirits to fill up."

Worried about Jefferson's continuing despair, in late November, his friends in the Continental Congress arranged to have him reappointed minister plenipotentiary [invested with full power] to go to France and negotiate the peace. Jefferson accepted. However, when it came time for him to sail, the French frigate that was to carry him lay frozen in the ice of Baltimore's harbor, and by the time it was possible to depart news arrived that a provisional treaty had already been signed. In April 1783, Congress cancelled Jefferson's appointment.

Disappointed at not getting to Paris, nevertheless, this experience had lifted Jefferson out of his gloom and recommitted him to the world of public affairs. In June, the Virginia Assembly elected him a delegate to Congress of the new Confederation of States, the weak central government established by the Articles of Confederation. Meeting in Annapolis during the winter of 1783–84, this Congress ratified the final peace treaty, and in a formal ceremony on December 23, 1783, accepted General Washington's resignation as commander in chief. Amidst tears, the general bade an affectionate farewell and began what he thought would be his final retirement from public life.

Jefferson would serve in Congress a mere six months. Yet in this brief period he headed a number of most important committees and drafted some 31 major reports. Some of these were of extraordinary importance, particularly his plans for the coinage and for the western territories.

America had no uniform currency at that time. The various states had their own currencies. Foreign coins also circulated widely, but with no agreed-upon value. In his report, "Notes on Coinage," Jefferson proposed a decimal plan, a simple system of currency based on 10s. "Everyone knows the facility of decimal arithmetic," he noted. "In all cases where we are free to choose between easy and difficult modes of operation, it is most rational to choose the easy." Congress adopted this uncomplicated system of coinage.

Even more consequential was Jefferson's plan for the western territory ceded to the United States by the states when the Articles of Confederation had been agreed to in 1781. Hardy settlers were already pushing into this vast land area between the Appalachians and the Mississippi River. Jefferson's report affirmed the principle that the western territories would be admitted as republican states on a basis of equality with the original 13 states. This was to take place in stages. Initially settlers would have the right to form a temporary government by adopting the constitution and laws of any of the original states. When a territory reached a population of 20,000, Congress was to authorize the calling of a constitutional convention to establish a permanent government. Finally, when population equaled that of the least populous of the original states, the new state would be admitted into the Union on an equal footing with the original states. Thus, unlike Great Britain, the United States would not create an exploitive empire with dependent colonies. Instead, they would establish what Jefferson called "an empire of liberty." First passed by Congress as the Land Ordinance of 1784, this became the basis for the more famous Northwest Ordinance of 1787.

Jefferson's report also proposed the prohibition of slavery in all western territories after the year 1800. The northern states supported him on this, but most southern delegates opposed it. The vote ended in a tie, effectively killing the measure. Three years later, however, the Northwest Ordinance, based on Jefferson's ideas, did outlaw slavery north of the Ohio River, giving at least a partial victory for the antislavery advocates (see chapter 9).

On May 7, 1784, Jefferson's service to the Confederation Congress ended abruptly. Congress appointed him to join Franklin and Adams to negotiate treaties of friendship and commerce with the European nations. Jefferson arranged for his eldest daughter, Patsy, and his favorite servant, James Hemings, to accompany him to Paris. His two youngest daughters, Mary (nicknamed Polly) and Lucy Elizabeth, were left in the care of his wife's sister Elizabeth Eppes. Since Jefferson's mission was to represent the commercial interest of all the states, he decided to sail from Boston so that he might tour New England where he had never been.

On July 5, Jefferson, Patsy, and Hemings departed from Boston on the *Ceres*, a new merchant sailing ship. They enjoyed a smooth and swift crossing, and on July 26 landed on the south coast of England. On the evening of July 30, they embarked on a rainy, rough Channel crossing to Le Havre. The next morning, they disembarked on French soil.

Anticipating his mission to last only a year or at most two, Jefferson would spend the next five years in Europe, mostly in Paris. It would be an eye-opening experience. He would converse with kings and revolutionaries, philosophers and farmers. And he would witness, and even participate in, the coming of the French Revolution—one of the most momentous events in human history.

4

AN AMERICAN IN PARIS

Jefferson arrived in Paris on August 6, 1784. Crossing the Seine River on the gracefully arched bridge, Pont de Neuilly, and riding down the elegant Champs-Élysées, he felt the charms of this ancient and magnificent Old World city. One of the first things Jefferson and his daughter did after settling in temporary lodgings was to shop for clothing. Both father and daughter abandoned their provincial attire for the latest Paris fashions. Jefferson even purchased lace ruffles for his sleeves and a decorative sword and belt with a silver buckle.

Soon after his arrival, Jefferson paid a call on Benjamin Franklin, who lived in a sumptuous estate in the village of Passy just outside Paris. Since 1776, Franklin had represented American interests in France and Europe. Now, at 78, he suffered from gout and a painful bladder stone that made it difficult for him to get around. Still his reputation as a scientist, statesman, wit, and inventor was so great that leading intellectuals and political figures regularly beat a path to his door. There was even a rage for Franklin souvenirs in France. One could buy busts, paintings, and miniature portraits of him set in the lids of snuffboxes and rings. Franklin's personal diplomacy during the course of the Revolution had gained French support for the American cause, a major factor in winning the war.

Jefferson revered Franklin, and the older man for his part liked and admired his junior colleague. Late in August, John Adams joined them, and soon these three giants of the Revolution, who had last come together to write the Declaration of Independence, began meeting regularly to try to negotiate commercial treaties with European states. Having broken Britain's political bondage, they now hoped that by opening new markets to American ships and products that British economic bondage could be broken as well. Their goal was to arrange free-trade treaties between the United States and the nations of Europe.

The three Americans, according to Adams, worked together "with wonderful harmony, good humor and unanimity." Yet despite weeks of thorough preparations, their negotiations yielded little. European governments were reluctant to sign a treaty with a nation so new and facing so uncertain a future. Eventually, Jefferson won some trade concessions from France, but only Frederick the Great of Prussia, Europe's most enlightened ruler, signed the treaty.

During this period, Jefferson became much closer to John Adams, his wife Abigail, and their son John Quincy, and daughter Nabby. Jefferson was often a dinner guest at their rented villa and reciprocated with his own dinner invitations after moving into more lavish quarters in October 1784. The Adamses, like Jefferson, were new to Paris, but, unlike the Virginian, took a rather prudish view of what they considered the decadence of Parisian society.

Franklin, on the other hand, relished the intrigues and flirtations of the city's elite. He introduced Jefferson to an accomplished society of philosophers, scientists, artists, and musicians. He accompanied the younger man to the salons of fashionable ladies where wit, wisdom, and music could be enjoyed. Not since his student days as a guest at the Governor's Palace had Jefferson experienced such scintillating social life.

Equally important to Jefferson in gaining entrée into the highest ranks of French society was his friendship with the Marquis de Lafayette. A hero of the American Revolution, Lafayette had returned a hero to the French as well. A nobleman with influence at court and connections with leading aristocrats, intellectuals, and political figures, Lafayette became a close and indispensable friend to Jefferson. At Lafayette's opulent Left Bank chateau opposite the Tuileries Palace, Jefferson met some of the most intelligent and influential men and women in France. As was the custom of that day,

Lafayette wrote letters of introduction for Jefferson, which virtually assured the American a warm welcome anywhere he traveled in France.

In January 1785, Jefferson learned that his two-year-old daughter, Lucy, had died of whooping cough. He took ill and spent much of the winter confined to bed. But spring returned and so did Jefferson's health and spirits. He began taking regular walks through the city and resumed his full social life.

By this time, he was enamored of French society. He wished Americans could be as well mannered as the French. "Here," he claimed, "a man might pass a life without encountering a single rudeness." He became a connoisseur of French wines and was pleased to find that despite the prevalence of wine drinking he had "never seen a man drunk in France, even among the lowest of the people." Jefferson also loved French cuisine—so much so that he sent his servant James Hemings out to study with a famous French chef. But he lavished his highest praise on French culture: "Were I to proceed to tell you how much I enjoy their architecture, sculpture, painting, music, I should want words. It is in these arts they shine."

Already admired as the author of the Declaration of Independence, Jefferson's reputation was further enhanced with the publication of his *Notes on the State of Virginia*. In the spring of 1785, Jefferson had 200 copies printed to circulate privately to friends in both France and America. But a French translation soon appeared, whereupon Jefferson authorized the publication of an English edition. *Notes* attracted wide attention in Europe and America and established the author as an enlightened intellectual of the first rank.

In May of 1785, the aged Franklin finally retired, and Jefferson replaced him as the sole American minister to France. At the same time, John Adams was posted to England as the first American ambassador to the Court of St. James. On May 17, Jefferson drove to the palace at Versailles to present himself before King Louis XVI and Queen Marie Antoinette. He liked the king but had little good to say about the "gaudily painted" queen. Jefferson would stay at this post for the next four years. Being away from America, he would be but a distant observer of events there that climaxed in the drafting of the Constitution in 1787. On the other hand, before departing for home in

October 1789, he would be an eyewitness and participant in the dramatic commencement of the French Revolution.

Ambassador Jefferson worked tirelessly to further American interests. He persuaded the French to accept an increased quota of American tobacco and to open French ports to the import of whale oil from New England. He sent back to friends in the States information on trade, commerce, scientific discoveries, and inventions. He shipped various European plants and animals that they might be introduced in America. To his friend James Madison he dispatched more than 200 books on political theory and history that would influence Madison's work on the new American Constitution. Jefferson also frequently assisted visiting Americans, including Thomas Paine, whom he helped obtain funding and patents for a new type of iron bridge.

As befit his ambassadorial status, he rented a handsome villa at the top of the Champs-Élysées, looking out at the English gardens of the Comtesse de Marbeuf. This house had all the latest gadgets, including running water pumped from the Seine River by steam engine and one of the first flush toilets. It also had stables, gardens, and extensive grounds. Here Jefferson entertained on a grand scale.

In the spring of 1786, Jefferson joined Adams in London in the hopes of signing a commercial treaty with Great Britain. Negotiations proved futile. When presented to King George III, whom Jefferson had so chastised in the Declaration of Independence, the king was barely civil.

Despite the diplomatic failure, Jefferson took advantage of what would be his one extended stay in England. He and Adams spent six weeks touring the famous gardens and factories of Great Britain. Jefferson particularly admired the naturalistic style of English gardens—more wild and picturesque than formal French gardens. English gardening, he wrote, "surpasses all the earth." He would later apply many ideas gleaned from his tour in landscaping Monticello. Jefferson also paid close attention to English steam engines and other machinery that was launching the Industrial Revolution. Yet while he admired the technological ingenuity, the "abject oppression" of the workers left him appalled. Overall, Jefferson found much more to dislike in England than to like, and he returned from his trip convinced that Britain was "the only nation on earth who wish us ill from the bottom of their soul."

While in London, Jefferson had met an American artist, John Trumbull, who was doing a series of historical paintings of the Revolution. Jefferson liked the young man, sat for a portrait, and invited Trumbull to stay with him when in Paris. The painter accepted the invitation, and while visiting the ambassador in August 1786 he introduced Jefferson to Maria Cosway.

A self-portrait of Maria Cosway, 1787. (Author's collection)

A 27-year-old English artist and musician who had been raised in Italy, Maria Cosway was a charming, flirtatious beauty. With "a mass of curly golden hair," bright blue eyes, an angelic face, and a languid voice that spoke English with a delightful Italian accent, Maria captivated numerous men. Almost at first sight of her, the usually reserved 43-year-old Jefferson was bowled over. He soon came to see in Maria the ideals he associated with femininity — "music, modesty, beauty, and that softness of disposition which is the ornament of her sex and charm of ours."

That day of their first meeting, Jefferson contrived to remain with Maria as long as possible. He cancelled a previous dinner engagement and took her, Trumbull, and various others off in his carriage to dine at an elegant restaurant in Saint-Cloud, between Paris and Versailles. "How beautiful was every object," Jefferson later reminisced, "the Pont de Neuilly, the hills along the Seine, the chateau, the gardens." After dinner, the party continued at a Parisian pleasure garden famous for its fireworks' displays, followed by a visit to the home of a celebrated Viennese harpist. Jefferson never forgot these adventures: "How well I remember them all," he confessed to Maria, "when I came home at night and looked back to the morning, it seemed to have been a month agone."

There was, however, one serious problem with this budding romance — Maria was married. Her husband, Richard Cosway, was a famed English miniaturist painter some three years older than Jefferson. A short, foppish, eccentric man known for his dissolute behavior, the marriage had not been a happy one. Flattered at Jefferson's attentions, Maria clearly encouraged him, and for the next several weeks after their first meeting the two conspired to spend as much time as possible together. It was a summer idyll and made Jefferson feel young again. Unfortunately too young, for on one exuberant occasion he playfully tried to leap a fence only to catch his foot and come down hard, breaking his right wrist. Improperly set, the wrist remained painful and drastically hampered his violin playing for the rest of his life.

In October 1786, Richard and Maria Cosway returned to London. Jefferson was heartbroken. In his most famous letter — a long epistle written with his left hand because of the broken wrist — he poured out to Maria the conflict within himself between his Head and his Heart. It is a classic dialogue of the clash between reason and feeling, reality and dreams. Head begins: "Well, friend, you seem to be in a pretty trim." To which Heart replies: "I am indeed the most wretched of all earthly beings." Head then chastises Heart and tells him that these feelings "are the eternal consequences of your warmth and precipitation. This is one of the scrapes into which you are ever leading us." Head continues: "Do not bite at the bait of pleasure, till you know there is no hook beneath it. The art of life is the art of avoiding pain. . . . The most effectual means of being secure against pain is to retire within ourselves, and to suffice for our own happiness." But Heart has the last word: "I feel more fit for death than life. But when I look back on the pleasures of which it is the consequence, I am conscious they were worth the price I am paying. . . . Hope is sweeter than despair, and they were too good to mean to deceive me. In the summer, said the gentleman; but in the spring, said the lady: and I should love her forever, were it only for that!"

Jefferson continued to write to Maria and longed for her return to Paris. To console himself he took an extended trip to the south of France and northern Italy. Leaving in late February 1787, he did not return to Paris until June. Reporting on the first part of his travels in a letter to his secretary William Short, he professed that "architecture, painting, sculpture, antiquities, agriculture, the condition of the labouring poor fill all my moments." Writing from Aix-en-Provence in late March, he exalted: "I am now in the land of corn, wine, oil, and sunshine. What more can man ask of heaven?"

In his travels Jefferson often stopped along country roads to question peasants working in the fields. He studied the different techniques for growing such crops as capers, grapes, and rice. He became fascinated with olives and shipped several dozen seedlings home to encourage their cultivation in America. Reaching the Piedmont of northern Italy after a precarious journey over the snowy Alps on mule, Jefferson smuggled out seed rice hidden in his overcoat even though removal of such rice was forbidden under penalty of death. He sent the rice to friends in the Carolinas to bolster rice production there. In Burgundy, Jefferson made arrangements with a wine merchant named Parent to ship wines to his Paris villa. Parent would remain Jefferson's principal wine broker ever after and the Virginian's instructions to him must have delighted the merchant: "Quality first, then price."

The three and a half months of travel did Jefferson a world of good. Near the end of his tour, he had written: "The plan of my journey as well as my life being to take things by the smooth handle, few things occur which have not something tolerable to offer me." Perhaps being away from the familiar places he had seen with Maria had given him time to reflect on the impossibility of the relationship. The head reasserted itself, and although Maria did return to Paris without her husband late in the summer of 1787, the joys of the previous summer were not repeated. She left Paris that December. Jefferson would never see her again.

But by then, pivotal political developments were absorbing the ambassador's attention. In November 1787, the month before Maria's departure, John Adams had sent Jefferson a copy of the newly written United States Constitution. Having been absent from America since 1784, Jefferson played only an indirect role in the events that had led to the calling of a Constitutional Convention held in Philadelphia in the summer of 1787. Since his days in the Confederation Congress, he had favored a stronger government. Through his letters he had impressed his views on his compatriots, particularly James Madison who played the most important role in drafting the new Constitution.

Reading the document, Jefferson approved of its general framework with the division of government into legislative, executive, and judicial branches. However, two things disturbed him—the absence of a specific bill of rights and the fact that there were no limits on the number of times a president could be reelected. To Jefferson, the perpetual reelectability of the president threatened to recreate monarchy. In letters to friends in America, he protested the president's reeligibility only to find that there were few concerned about this since everyone assumed that the highly trusted George Washington would be elected president. Jefferson soon abandoned this crusade, and not until 1951 would a constitutional amendment be adopted placing a two-term limit on the presidency.

The omission of a bill of rights struck the ambassador as an even more serious matter. The Federalists, those who had drafted the Constitution, felt no need for a such a bill, since the new government would have no power in the sphere of personal liberties. However, Anti-Federalists, the name given to those opposing the Constitution, used the absence of a bill of rights to rally resistance to ratification. Jefferson, while a Federalist in that he supported the Constitution, found personal liberties too fundamental to be left to inference. In a series of letters to Madison he urged the necessity of

> a bill of rights, providing clearly . . . for freedom of religion, freedom of the press, protection against standing armies, restriction of monopolies, the eternal and unremitting force of habeas corpus laws, and trials by jury in all matters of fact triable by the laws of the land. . . . A bill of rights is what the people are entitled to against every government on earth . . . and what no just government should refuse, or rest on inference.

Convinced by Jefferson's arguments, Madison drafted a bill of rights and led the crusade that would lead to the adoption of the first 10 amendments to the Constitution. Thus, Jefferson, far removed from the American scene, made a major contribution to the creation of a constitution that guaranteed the most basic human rights. With the addition of the Bill of Rights, he came to see the Constitution as the "wisest" form of government ever devised.

Jefferson had to be content to learn belatedly from friends' letters of the struggle over ratification and the eventual establishment of a new government under the Constitution. But increasingly his attention focused on rapidly unfolding events propelling France toward revolution. Shortly before Jefferson left Paris in February 1787 for his tour of southern France, he had attended the opening session of the Assembly of Notables at Versailles. The Assembly, composed of the leading nobles, clergy, and magistrates, had not met in more than a century and a half, but King Louis XVI called it in the hopes of solving an acute financial crisis and widespread discontent that plagued the nation.

By the time Jefferson returned in June, he saw reason to hope. Writing to Adams that August, he claimed that "in the course of three months the royal authority has lost, and the rights of the nation gained, as much ground, by a revolution of public opinion only, as England gained in all her civil wars under the Stuarts."

Early in 1788, America's own financial problems necessitated Jefferson traveling to Holland to join Adams in negotiating loans from Dutch bankers. This successfully accomplished, he took a leisurely trip through the German Rhineland before returning to France in late April. There he found that the "gay and thoughtless Paris is now become a furnace of politics." That summer there was rioting in the city's streets. In September, the king's hated Swiss Guards killed several protestors. Only after the king declared martial law and promised to summon the Estates General—the historic national assembly of France—to meet early in 1789 was a degree of calm restored.

Throughout this period Jefferson consulted frequently with Lafayette, who was a member of the Assembly of Notables and the leader of those pushing for major reforms. Jefferson cautioned his friend to work for change within the system and to try to achieve a constitutional monarchy such as Great Britain's. This might seem strange advice coming from an American revolutionary. But Jefferson correctly judged the French situation to be different from the American. France, after all, had been a monarchy for over 1,000 years and feudal institutions remained intact. Having talked with many French peasants in his travels, he did not see them as ready for republican government. "They are not yet ripe for receiving the blessings to which they are entitled," he wrote Madison. But he believed that a positive transformation was occurring: "The nation has been awakened by our revolution. They feel their strength, they are enlightened, their lights are spreading and they will not retrograde."

When the Estates General finally assembled in Versailles on May 4, 1789, public expectations ran high. Composed of three separate orders—the First Estate, made up of clergy; the Second Estate, the nobles; and the Third Estate, representing the rest of the French people—at first the Estates General deadlocked over whether voting would be by separate Estates or as a single assembly. Many of the more liberal nobles such as Lafayette and some of the clergy supported the idea of joining with the Third Estate and forming a unified assembly. But most of the nobles and clergy balked at relinquishing their privileged positions. Frustrated at this intransigence, on June 17, the Third Estate proclaimed itself the National Assembly of France.

Jefferson, who had traveled to Versailles almost daily to observe the proceedings, now wrote, "The fate of the nation depends on the conduct of the King and his ministers. Were they to side openly with the commons, the revolution would be completely without a convulsion. A constitution would result, totally free and in which the distinction of noble and commoner would be suppressed." On June 27, King Louis XVI requested the nobles and clergy to take their seats with the Third Estate in the National Assembly. Spontaneous popular demonstrations erupted. Jefferson elatedly but naively noted that "this great crisis [is] now over."

During this exhilarating period, Jefferson had been secretly working with Lafayette to draw up a declaration of rights to be adopted by the National Assembly. The two studied the Declaration of Independence and the Virginia declaration of rights. Jefferson suggested to his friend giving each generation the right "to examine and, if necessary, to modify the form of government." On July 4, these two and other friends joined in celebrating the 13th anniversary of American independence.

But Jefferson's optimism that a peaceful revolution was taking place proved short-lived. On July 12, angry mobs attacked and burned the Customs House, a hated symbol of taxation that stood just across the street from Jefferson's house. The people of Paris, he wrote that night, "now armed themselves with such weapons as they could find in armorers' shops and private houses and were roaming all night through all parts of the city."

Two days later, crowds of demonstrators stormed the Bastille, the fortress where the government traditionally held political prisoners. Lafayette now took command of the Paris Guard, forcing the Swiss Guard and other foreign mercenaries (soldiers-for-hire) to flee. On July 17, Jefferson stood at his balcony as Lafayette and his armed guard together with about 60,000 citizens marched down the Champs-Élysées surrounding the royal carriage bearing King Louis XVI. "People in the streets, doors and windows," Jefferson reported, "saluted them everywhere with cries of 'vive la nation.'"

The Revolution appeared to be won. In late July, the National Assembly adopted the Declaration of Rights (Declaration of the Rights of Man and the Citizen) that Jefferson had helped write. By early August, he praised the Assembly for abolishing "all titles of rank, all the abusive privileges of feudalism." Jefferson felt fortunate "to see in the course of fourteen years two such revolutions as were never before seen." He realized that he had witnessed "such events as will be for ever memorable in history."

Yet he did not really grasp the nature of the tumult taking place around him and persisted in seeing the French Revolution as a constitutional reformation, failing to comprehend the immense social upheaval simmering after centuries of injustice. Very wise in American ways, he was naive about things French. He never completely understood the vast difference between the social situations in the United States and France. Convinced that the situation had stabilized under the "wise, firm and moderate" leadership of the National Assembly, Jefferson decided to take a six-month recess from his diplomatic post. Not realizing that the Revolution was really only beginning, he left Paris in late September 1789, satisfied that he had witnessed "but the first chapter in the history of European liberty."

5

FEDERALISTS AND REPUBLICANS

On November 23, 1789, Jefferson landed at Norfolk, Virginia, and set foot on American soil for the first time in more than five years. He intended to spend six months at Monticello and then return to his post in Paris the following spring. But soon after his arrival, he learned that President George Washington had appointed him secretary of state in the new government under the Constitution and that the Senate had already approved his nomination. Still wishing to go back to France, he was reluctant to accept. In letters and through emissaries the president flattered and urged his fellow Virginian. It proved hard for Jefferson to reject his request, and finally in mid-February 1790, he agreed to take the position. He would never see his beloved France again.

A happy event delayed Jefferson's taking leave of Monticello. On February 23, following a whirlwind courtship, Patsy, Jefferson's 17-year-old daughter, married Thomas Mann Randolph, Jr., her third cousin and the son of Jefferson's old playmate from his childhood days at Tuckahoe. Pronouncing the young Randolph a "gentleman of genius, science, and honorable mind," Jefferson bestowed 25 slaves and 1,000 acres on the newlyweds.

On March 1, Jefferson left Monticello to take up his new post. Stopping in Philadelphia en route to pay his last respects to the dying Benjamin Franklin, it was not until March 21 that he reached New York City, the temporary capital. The new government that Jefferson joined had been in operation slightly less than a year and its success was by no means assured. The fight over ratifying the Constitution had been bitter and close and many people did not wish the new government well. Yet by the time Jefferson associated himself with the fledgling experiment, Congress had passed the Bill of Rights, swelling the popularity of the Constitution. Equally important in winning support for the government and its Constitution was the fact that General Washington, the great hero of the Revolution, served as president. Washington's popularity lent authenticity to the government. Observing this, Jefferson optimistically claimed that "the opposition to our new constitution has almost totally disappeared."

New York City, with a population of 33,000, struck Jefferson as provincial after the grandeur of Paris, which had some 600,000 inhabitants. Unlike the great villa he had enjoyed in France, he had to settle for a small house on Maiden Lane, in lower Manhattan. But it was the city's political climate that most disturbed him. "I had left France in the first year of her revolution, in the fervor of natural rights and zeal for reformation," he recalled. "My conscientious devotion to these rights . . . had been aroused and excited by daily exercise." In New York City, however, he was astounded to discover that "a preference of kingly, over republican government was evidently the favorite sentiment." The president, other high-ranking officials, and eminent New Yorkers hosted the new cabinet member at a number of dinner parties. But time and again, Jefferson found himself "the only advocate on the republican side."

Living amidst the political ferment in France, Jefferson remained unaware of the conservative reaction that had taken place in his own country. In the mid-1770s, alarmed at British violations of American rights, many notable citizens had thrown their support behind the Declaration of Independence and the fight for republican liberties. But once independence had been achieved, many of these individuals had become frightened by what they saw as an excess of popular government. Such people hoped that the new government under the Constitution could create order and stability and curtail the influence of the people.

The very tone of the Washington administration struck Jefferson as "not at all in character with the simplicity of republican government, and looking as if wistfully to those of European courts." President Washington presided over highly formal weekly receptions, and on official public appearances he rode in a six-horse coach, accompanied by four uniformed servants and two gentlemen riders. The Senate suggested that the president be given the title "His Highness the President of the United States and Protector of Their Liberties." Even Jefferson's old friend John Adams, who was vice president, argued that without "splendor and majesty" neither "dignity nor authority" could be preserved.

Soon Jefferson came to see a connection between the aristocratic social atmosphere and the policies being advanced by a fellow cabinet member, Alexander Hamilton, the secretary of

Painting of Alexander Hamilton by John Trumbull (The Frick Art Reference Library)

the treasury. "Hamilton," Jefferson would later claim, "was not only a monarchist, but for a monarchy bottomed on corruption. . . . Hamilton was, indeed, a singular character. Of acute understanding, disinterested, honest and honorable in all private transactions, amiable in society, and duly valuing virtue in private life, yet so bewitched and perverted by the British example, as to be under thorough conviction that corruption was essential to the government of a nation."

Unlike Jefferson, who was born to wealth and high social standing, Hamilton came from an obscure West Indian background and was orphaned and apprenticed in a store before he was 13. Bright, ambitious, and discontent at the prospect of spending his life in "the grovelling condition of a clerk," at the age of 16 he made his way to New York City, and in 1772 entered King's College, now Columbia University. While still a student in his teens, he wrote clever pamphlets supporting the colonists' cause, and when the Revolution broke out he attached himself to General Washington, becoming his military secretary and aide-de-camp. In 1780, he married Elizabeth Schuyler and thus tied his future to one of the most prominent families in New York State. During the 1780s, he served in Congress, practiced law, and played a role in drafting the Constitution and fighting for its ratification. In the spring of 1790, when Jefferson arrived on the scene, Hamilton, some 12 years younger than the Virginian, was already recognized as the most powerful figure in Washington's government.

Like many self-made men, Hamilton disdained the mass of humanity that he had risen above. He referred to the people as "a great beast," irrational, prone to violence, and needing a strong government to keep them under control. At the Constitutional Convention, he had proposed having a president and senate chosen for life. Failing in this, he set about to do everything in his power to assure the dominance of "the rich and well born" over "the mass of the people" in order to check what he termed "the imprudence of democracy." He hoped to do this by funding all government obligations, thereby fusing the concerns of wealthy creditors with the interests of the government.

The first part of Hamilton's plan had already been adopted before Jefferson arrived. His Report on the Public Credit (January 1790) called for funding the national debt incurred during the Revolution. Although the paper certificates issued during the war had been circulating at only a fraction of their printed worth, Hamilton's plan called for redeeming this debt at face value. Despite the fact that speculators stood to profit handsomely by this measure, Congress approved.

However, a second part of Hamilton's plan was still pending when Jefferson took office. Hamilton had proposed that the federal government assume the state debts as well and thus cement the financial interests of state creditors with the national government while at the same time weakening state power. In Congress this proposition stirred heated debate. Some of the states, including Virginia, had paid off most of their debts; whereas other states, particularly in New England, still had large debts. The bill passed in the Senate, but lost by two votes in the House.

Soon after this setback, a dejected Hamilton ran into the recently arrived Jefferson outside Washington's door on Broadway. Since opposition to the assumption of the state debts was strongest in the South, the New Yorker appealed to the Virginian for help. Jefferson agreed to host a dinner for Hamilton and James Madison the following evening. At that gathering they worked out a deal. Jefferson promised that he would persuade two Virginia congressmen to change their votes to favor the assumption bill. In return, Hamilton pledged to win northern support to establish the permanent capital along the Potomac River in the South.

The compromise held, and in July 1790 Congress passed the debt-assumption act and acceded to locating the permanent national capital along the Potomac after a 10-year stopover in Philadelphia. At the time, Jefferson did not fully grasp the implications of Hamilton's far-reaching plan. Later he would claim that Hamilton had "duped" him and made him a "tool for forwarding his schemes, not then sufficiently understood by me."

When Congress adjourned in August 1790, Jefferson returned home. Traveling with Madison, they stopped in Georgetown to inspect possible sites for the future capital. After a relaxing autumn at Monticello, Jefferson returned to his State Department duties in November. His job was now in Philadelphia, where he had made arrangements to rent a pleasant house on Market Street close to the State Department offices. There he unpacked some 78 large crates of goods he had purchased in Paris, containing quantities of furniture and books, dozens of cases of wine, paintings and statues, and even two cases of macaroni, a food he had come to love during his tour of Italy. He persuaded his French butler, Adrien Petit, to come head his household staff and once again had his slave James Hemings in his kitchen to serve up French food.

Jefferson liked Philadelphia, then the largest city in America. He had friends there from his days in the Continental Congress, and it was the home of the American Philosophical Society, the country's foremost scientific and philosophical organization and the closest America could come to a Parisian-type intellectual salon. Jefferson, already a member, would be elected vice president of the Society that January. He loved intellectual inquiry; however, politics and the duties of his office left scarce time for scientific projects.

When Congress reconvened that December, Hamilton submitted a Report on the National Bank that would bring to a boil the already simmering conflict between Jefferson and the treasury secretary. Hamilton admired the English system of government and envisioned a bank of the United States as serving a function similar to the Bank of England. The bank would be the depository for government funds and issue paper money. This, he believed, would make more capital available for commerce and manufacturing. Finally, his proposed bank would once again tie the fortunes of the well-to-do with those of the government. Four-fifths of the bank's stock would be held by private investors and the remainder by the government.

Jefferson suspected that the proposed bank would promote moneyed interests at the expense of farmers and workers. It would further enrich wealthy merchants and industrialists and give them undo influence on the government. He also saw the bank as unconstitutional. Madison, Jefferson's closest ally, led the fight against the bank bill in Congress but failed to block its passage. In February 1791, the bill was sent to Washington. Before signing it, the president asked for opinions on its constitutionality from Edmund Randolph, the attorney general, and from Jefferson and Hamilton. Randolph sent the first memo to Washington, declaring the bank unconstitutional.

Jefferson agreed, and in an influential paper argued for what came to be called a "strict construction" of the Constitution.

Citing the 10th Amendment that "the powers not delegated to the United States by the Constitution, nor prohibited by it to the States, are reserved to the States respectively, or to the people," Jefferson reasoned that "to take a single step beyond the boundaries thus specially drawn around the powers of Congress, is to take possession of a boundless field of power, no longer susceptible of any definition." Therefore, since chartering a bank was not among the powers enumerated by the Constitution, such a measure was clearly unconstitutional.

Hamilton disagreed. Having had the advantage of reading Randolph's and Jefferson's briefs before writing his own, he asserted a "loose construction" of the Constitution. The gauge of what is constitutional and what is not, he reasoned, "is the *end* to which the measure relates as a *means*. If the end be clearly comprehended within any of the specified powers, and if the measure have an obvious relation to that end, and is not forbidden by any particular provision of the constitution — it may safely be deemed to come within the compass of national authority."

Hamilton's arguments persuaded Washington, and he signed the bank bill into law. A loose construction of the Constitution prevailed and national authority expanded. Hamilton and those whom Jefferson contemptuously referred to as "stockjobbers" emerged victorious. But conflict over the nature of the Constitution was far from over.

By this time, Congress splintered into two distinct factions. Madison galvanized opposition to Hamilton in the House. Another disciple of Jefferson, James Monroe, took the lead in the Senate. Claiming to speak for the people as opposed to the privileged, they called themselves Republicans or Democratic-Republicans. Partisans of Hamilton's programs took the name Federalists, a term originally used to designate supporters of the Constitution. Political parties were taking shape.

To Jefferson, this represented a "contest of principle, between the advocates of republican, and those of kingly government." Yet as a member of Washington's cabinet, he was reluctant to appear publicly as the leader of the party opposing the secretary of treasury. In May 1791, however, Jefferson's dissent inadvertently became public knowledge.

A Philadelphia printer planning to publish Thomas Paine's revolutionary treatise, *The Rights of Man*, loaned Jefferson a copy. Returning the work, Jefferson added a note stating that he was pleased Paine's pamphlet was to be published in the capital and that "something is at length to be publicly said against the political heresies which have sprung up among us. I have no doubt our citizens will rally a second time round the standard of Common Sense." When *Rights of Man* was published in May 1791, Jefferson was astounded to see his letter printed on the cover page. Newspapers quickly reprinted the note and Jefferson emerged in the public mind as the apostle of republicanism, combating Hamilton and the special interests.

That summer, Jefferson and Madison persuaded the radical poet Philip Freneau to establish a newspaper in Philadelphia. Their aim was to counteract Federalist editor John Fenno's *Gazette of the United States*, a paper that in Jefferson's words disseminated "the doctrines of monarchy, aristocracy and the exclusion of the influence of the people." Jefferson appointed Freneau to a $250-a-year post as a part-time translator in the State Department as well as promising him State Department printing jobs. With this support, in October 1791, Freneau launched the *National Gazette*.

The pro-Jeffersonian editor wasted no time in assaulting Hamilton and his followers. Infuriated, the secretary of treasury, under a variety of pen names, wrote scathing attacks on Jefferson that he published in Fenno's paper. Jefferson refused to directly involve himself in the fray, but his friend Madison contributed a number of unsigned articles to Freneau's *Gazette*. Quickly this escalated into a full-fledged newspaper war that spread from Philadelphia throughout the country and helped speed the emergence of a two-party system.

Washington took alarm. He, like most of the founding fathers, assumed that effective republican government would be consensual. The well-publicized conflict between two of his cabinet members caused him to fear for the future of the government. In the summer of 1792, the president sent confidential letters to Jefferson and Hamilton beseeching them to settle their disputes. It was reprehensible, he declared, that while the new nation stood surrounded by enemies "internal dissensions should be harrowing and tearing our vitals."

In their replies to Washington, both Jefferson and Hamilton blamed one another. Jefferson called Hamilton's policies "adverse to liberty" and "calculated to undermine and demolish the Republic." Hamilton himself he described as "a man whose history, from the moment at which history can stoop to notice him, is a tissue of machinations against the liberty of the country which has not only received and given him bread but heaped its honors on his head."

In his letter, Hamilton claimed to be the injured party: "I *know* that I have been an object of uniform opposition from Mr. Jefferson, from the first moment of his coming to the City of New York to enter upon his present office." Neither man gave any indication that they would alter their ways and the newspaper war raged on. Under the pen name "Catullus," Hamilton called Jefferson an "intriguing incendiary." Madison and Monroe countered with a series of six articles appearing under the title "Vindication of Mr. Jefferson."

That fall, the feuding factions contended for the first time in presidential and congressional elections. Neither Republicans nor Federalists wished to risk putting forth their own candidate for the presidency. In surprising agreement, Hamilton and Jefferson convinced Washington that he should stay on as president for another term in order to assure national unity. However, the Republicans did challenge the incumbent vice president, John Adams. Madison and Monroe organized support for Governor George Clinton of New York, a staunch opponent of Hamilton. Although Adams won, Clinton garnered unanimous electoral blocs in New York, North Carolina, and Georgia. The alliance between New York and the South would form the backbone of the Democratic-Republicans and eventually would send Jefferson to the White House as the nation's third president. Republicans were even more successful in the 1792 congressional elections. Jefferson saw the results as "generally in favor of republican and against the aristocratical candidates." With "a decided majority in favor of the republican interest" in the next Congress, Jefferson prophesied a rapid return to "the true principles of the Constitution."

Jefferson had hoped to retire at the end of Washington's first term. He pined for Monticello "with the fondness of a sailor who has land in view." However, the persistent assaults on his character by Hamilton and other Federalists made him reluctant to resign for fear of appearing to retreat from the battle.

In February 1793, he assured Washington that he would stay on at least for the time being.

Seventeen ninety-three proved to be one of the most trying years in Jefferson's political life. The Reign of Terror swept France as a general war engulfed Europe. At home, political divisions sharpened and grew more acrimonious. A yellow fever epidemic scourged Philadephia, killing thousands of people and forcing the government to flee the city.

The year opened with the news that the newly declared French Republic had defeated the invading forces of Prussia. Jubilation swept America. Jefferson reported "universal feasts and rejoicings." However, in March when Americans learned of the execution of King Louis XVI and that France had declared war on Britain, Spain, and Holland, enthusiasm for the French Revolution waned, particularly among Federalists. Indeed the war in Europe soon became a major factor in dividing Americans into opposing political parties. As Jefferson noted, the international conflict "kindled and brought forward the two parties with an ardor which our own interests merely could never incite."

Hamilton and the Federalists wished for closer ties with England and had no desire that the United States should honor its 1778 treaty with France. Hamilton accused Republicans of having "a womanish attachment to France."

Jefferson, for his part, never flinched in his support for the French Revolution. He regarded its success as indispensable to the spread of liberty. Were the Revolution in France checked, he maintained, it "would retard the revival of liberty in other countries. I consider the establishment and success of their government as necessary to stay up our own and to prevent it from falling back to that kind of Half-way-house, the English constitution." Even as the Revolution became more violent and some of his former French friends were put to death, Jefferson remained steadfast in his support: "The liberty of the whole earth was depending on the issue of the contest, and was ever such a prize won with so little innocent blood?"

Americans celebrated when the first minister of the French Republic, Citizen Edmond Charles Genêt, arrived in Charleston, South Carolina, on April 8, 1793. Hamilton, however, tried to persuade Washington not to receive the French minister and to abrogate the treaty of 1778 with France since that had been made with the monarchy and not the republic. He asked the president to declare American neutrality, a policy that favored the British since they dominated the seas.

Jefferson was placed in a difficult situation. He was bent on taking no action that implied opposition to the principles of the French Revolution or the repudiation of the French alliance. Yet at the same time, he did not wish to see America involved in European wars. Over Hamilton's objections, he persuaded Washington to receive Genêt and to recognize the legitimacy of the 1778 treaty. He also successfully urged Washington to avoid using the word *neutrality* in proclaiming America's non-involvement. He hoped that this would minimize the offense to France and leave the door open for later commercial concessions from Britain.

However, the actions of the exuberant Genêt quickly undermined Jefferson's pro-French position. Received with popular enthusiasm in his travels from Charleston to Philadelphia, Genêt assumed that the American people overwhelmingly supported the French cause. He had difficulty understanding the government's unwillingness to offer military assistance and the cool reception President Washington accorded him. In defiance of American neutrality, Genêt began outfitting privateers and recruiting Americans for military service both at sea and on land against the Spanish who controlled Florida. Even before Genêt reached Philadelphia, French privateers captured several British merchant ships and brought them into American ports to be sold as prizes of war. These violations of American sovereignty embarrassed Jefferson and fanned the anti-French fires of the Federalists.

The president ordered French privateers out of American waters. Jefferson repeated this demand and warned Genêt to avoid all further violations of American neutrality. Contemptuous of Washington, and feeling that Jefferson was only expressing the administration's position and not his own, Genêt continued his actions. Blithely ignoring the government, he appealed directly to the American people in an undiplomatic effort to undermine the Washington administration. Jefferson's patience gave out. "Never," he fumed, "was so calamitous an appointment made." In August 1793, he joined with Hamilton and the rest of the cabinet in demanding the French minister's recall.

The Genêt affair was a bitter experience for Jefferson. Federalists made political capital in criticizing his pro-French position. In the midst of the crisis, the secretary of state had informed Washington of his intention to retire "from the hated occupation of politics" by the end of September. Washington once again persuaded him to stay on until the end of the year. His political fortunes seemingly at a low ebb, on December 31, 1793, Jefferson resigned his office. Now in his 51st year, he determined never again to return to public life.

6

"THE REVOLUTION OF 1800"

In early January 1794, Thomas Jefferson left Philadelphia for Monticello. "My farm, my family and my books call me to them irresistibly," he wrote. To his cousin Edmund Randolph, who succeeded him as secretary of state, he confessed: "I cherish tranquillity too much to suffer political things to enter my mind at all." He gave up reading newspapers and became what he described as "the most ardent and active farmer in the state. I live constantly on horseback, rarely taking a book and never a pen if I can avoid it." Jefferson had always idealized farming. Now in his 50s, he could truly enjoy the pastoral idyll. "How much better this," he boasted, "than to be shut up in the four walls of an office, the sun ever excluded."

Yet years of public service away from Monticello had left his lands depleted. At the time of his retirement, Jefferson owned more than 10,000 acres. About half of this lay some 80 miles to the southwest at a plantation called Poplar Forest. This property was under the supervision of a trusted manager, and Jefferson rarely went there. He concentrated his efforts on the lands in Albemarle County on both sides of the Rivanna River and contiguous to Monticello. Here decades of tobacco planting under a succession of indifferent overseers had exhausted the soil. In place of tobacco, Jefferson implemented a system of crop rotation, planting wheat, peas, corn, potatoes, and clover. In

Through mathematical principles, Thomas Jefferson designed this mold-board plow. The Agricultural Society of Paris awarded him a gold medal for his design. (National Museum of American History, Smithsonian Institution)

addition to improving the soil, such crops supplied food and required less labor than tobacco.

As part of his effort to modernize his farms and make them more efficient, Jefferson experimented with labor-saving devices. He built a gristmill, and to streamline wheat harvesting he designed a compact horse-powered threshing machine. His most celebrated invention was an improved moldboard plow. Through a mathematical formula that still governs the shape of plowshares, Jefferson devised a plow of least resistance that gradually raised and turned over the turf. Attracting considerable attention from scientists as well as farmers, the French National Institute of Agriculture awarded him a gold medal for his design.

Jefferson considered his various inventions and improvements public property. He never took out patents nor made money from them. However, to supplement his farming income he established a shop to manufacture nails. By 1796, the shop was producing about a ton of nails a month. Its workers consisted of a dozen young male slaves aged 10 to 16 whom Jefferson had trained and continued to supervise.

During this period of retirement, Jefferson also turned his attention to extensively remodeling and enlarging Monticello.

This project would take many years and result in the mansion that remains to this day (see chapter 8).

But much as Jefferson reveled in the life of "a real farmer, measuring fields, following my ploughs, helping the haymakers," such bucolic bliss could not last. Despite his best efforts to avoid the public arena, the turbulence of domestic and international politics could not long be kept at bay. Only eight months into his retirement, Washington asked him to go as a special envoy to negotiate with Spain; he steadfastly refused. When his closest political associate James Madison urged him to become the Republican candidate for the presidency in 1796, Jefferson replied that the "little spice of ambition which I had in my younger days has long since evaporated."

Yet his letters to friends indicate Jefferson's increasing political concerns. When Alexander Hamilton persuaded Washington to place him at the head of a large federal force to crush Pennsylvania farmers opposing a new excise tax on whiskey, Jefferson protested the excessive use of the military. When the president admonished the Democratic societies that had sprung up in support of the French Revolution and the Republican cause, Jefferson denounced this as "an attack on the freedom of discussion, the freedom of writing, printing, and publishing." Jefferson condemned John Jay's treaty with England as an "infamous act, which is really nothing more than a treaty of alliance between England and the Anglomen [Anglophiles] of this country against the legislature and people of the United States."

In 1796, over his objections, Madison, Monroe, and other Republican leaders put Jefferson forth as their presidential candidate. His opponent in this first political party battle for the presidency was his old friend John Adams. Jefferson never left Monticello. Nor did Adams campaign. Nevertheless, it became a combative and close contest. Republicans touted Jefferson as the "steadfast friend of the rights of the people" and defamed Adams as an "advocate for hereditary power." Federalists for their part slandered Jefferson as a pro-French radical intent on overthrowing the government.

In the end, Adams, with 71 electoral votes, won the presidency by the slim margin of 3 votes over Jefferson's 68. Federalist Adams carried New England, New York, New Jersey, and Delaware. Republican Jefferson dominated in

Pennsylvania and the South, but lost single votes in North Carolina, Virginia, and Pennsylvania, providing Adams the margin of victory.

Until 1804, the Constitution failed to provide separate balloting for president and vice president, specifying instead that the candidate with the second highest electoral vote assumed the second office. Thus, for the only time in American history, the head of the opposition party became the vice president of the leader of the victorious party. It would not prove a pleasant experience for Jefferson.

At first, however, Jefferson accepted the second spot with equanimity. Despite their political differences, he still admired Adams and saw him as "the only sure barrier against Hamilton getting in." Accepting the vice presidency, Jefferson confided: "I can particularly have no feelings which would revolt at a secondary position to Mr. Adams. I am his junior in life, was his junior in Congress, his junior in the diplomatic line, his junior lately in the civil government."

The relationship began cordially. Arriving in Philadelphia on March 2, 1797, Jefferson immediately visited the president-elect. Adams returned the call the next day, and on March 4 the two old comrades marched into the House chamber and took the oath of office.

From Jefferson's perspective, an even higher honor befell him when the day before his inauguration as vice president he became the third president of the American Philosophical Society, succeeding the late eminent scientist David Rittenhouse, who in turn had followed the society's founder, Benjamin Franklin. Jefferson presented the society with the fossil bones of an ancient mammoth recently discovered in the western part of Virginia. He cherished the honor of heading the nation's preeminent scientific and philosophical society and would remain in that post until 1815.

His only recognized duty as vice president was to preside over the Senate. Since Congress was not in session at the time of Jefferson's inauguration, he soon left Philadelphia and returned to Monticello where he hoped to remain until Congress reconvened in December. These plans were interrupted when in May President Adams called a special session of Congress to deal with a crisis ignited by France's refusal to receive the newly appointed American Minister to France, Charles Cotesworth Pinckney.

Arriving back in Philadelphia, Jefferson found himself the center of controversy. A private letter that he had written to an Italian friend more than a year earlier had been printed in Italy, then translated into French and published in Paris, from which it was rendered back into English and published in a New York Federalist paper. Written during the controversy over the Jay Treaty, Jefferson's letter complained that republican government had been displaced by "an Anglican monarchical and aristocratical party . . . whose avowed object is to draw over us the substance, as they have already done the forms, of the British government." In the French version of the letter and the English translation published in New York, a sentence had been added charging Americans with ingratitude and injustice toward France. Jefferson had not written this; nevertheless, as tensions between the United States and France intensified, he came under sharp attack in the press.

The Jay Treaty appeared to the French to unite the Americans with Britain. In retaliation, French ships began plundering U.S. merchant vessels. Pro-English Federalists spoiled for a fight. President Adams charged the French with violating American sovereignty and urged Congress to show the French that the Americans were not "the miserable instruments of foreign influence." Congress quickly voted to build a navy and fortify the coast. An undeclared naval war erupted. In a last effort to settle matters peaceably, Adams appointed a three-person commission to attempt negotiations with the French. For the time being this defused the crisis.

In April 1798, the results of the mission to France became known when Congress published the commission's dispatches detailing the so-called XYZ affair. French agents, their names encoded as X, Y, and Z in the congressional report, had demanded an apology from President Adams, a loan, and a large bribe as the price for even meeting with the American envoys. The French government had further ordered the seizure of all neutral ships carrying enemy goods. War fever swept the nation. Congress hastened the buildup of the navy, armed merchant ships, authorized the capture of French vessels, and established a large army to be headed by Washington with

Hamilton as second in command. To pay for all this, new direct taxes were levied.

As the pro-French party, the Republicans bore the brunt of the anti-French hysteria. Rumors abounded. Federalist papers conjectured French troops landing in the South aided by traitorous Republicans. In Philadelphia, proadministration youths wearing black hats battled pro-French youths wearing the tricolored cockade of the French Revolution. Political passions boiled over. Jefferson noted how "men who have been intimate all their lives, cross the streets to avoid meeting, and turn their heads another way, lest they should be obliged to touch their hats." Fighting even broke out in the halls of Congress. Adams and Jefferson no longer consulted one another.

Under the guise of national security, the Federalists saw an opportunity to crush the Republican opposition once and for all. In July 1798, by a narrow margin, Federalists pushed through Congress alien and sedition laws. Directed against French and Irish immigrants particularly, the Alien Act empowered the president to deport any foreigner deemed "dangerous to the peace and safety of the United States" or any suspected of "treasonable or secret machinations against the government."

The Sedition Act aimed to quell domestic dissent and, in complete violation of the Bill of Rights, made it a federal crime to publish "any false, scandalous and malicious writing" against the government or its officials. This act launched what Jefferson called the "Federalist reign of terror." The first person convicted was Matthew Lyon, a Republican congressman from Vermont. Lyon had printed a statement saying that he could not support President Adams when he saw "every consideration of the public welfare swallowed up in a continual grasp for power, in an unbounded thirst for ridiculous pomp, foolish adulation and selfish avarice." All told some 25 persons were arrested, 14 indicted, and 10 convicted; all except Lyon were Republican newspaper editors, printers, and writers.

Although appalled, Jefferson had confidence that the people would not long tolerate the evils of oppressive laws, a standing army, and direct taxes. "A little patience," he wrote, "and we shall see the reign of witches pass over, their spells dissolved, and the people recovering their true sight, restoring the government to its true principles."

In his public roll as vice president, there was little Jefferson could do. But as the leader of the opposition party he decided to take action. He feared that the Alien and Sedition Acts were "merely an experiment on the American mind to see how far it will bear an avowed violation of the Constitution. If this goes down, we shall immediately see attempted another act of Congress, declaring that the President shall continue in office during life."

In secret, he drafted a resolution declaring the Alien and Sedition Acts unconstitutional. The state of Kentucky adopted Jefferson's resolution. Virginia adopted a similar declaration drawn up by Madison. The Kentucky and Virginia resolutions argued that the Union was a compact among the states and that all powers not specifically delegated to the national government remained with the states. "Whensoever the general government assumes undelegated powers, its acts are unauthoritative, void, and of no force."

Over time, these resolutions would be used by defenders of slavery to assert the doctrines of states' rights and nullification. But in 1798, the Kentucky and Virginia resolutions aimed solely at upholding basic civil liberties that were guaranteed by the Constitution. Directed against the Federalist administration of John Adams and the Federalist-controlled Congress, these resolutions also launched the presidential election campaign of 1800.

A reluctant political participant in 1796, by 1798 Jefferson had taken over the reins of leadership of the Republican Party. Through extensive correspondence, he helped weld the grassroots Republican organizations into an effective national party. Aware of the need to publicize the Republican cause, in 1799, a year before the election, Jefferson wrote to Madison: "We are sensible that this summer is the season for systematic energies and sacrifices. The engine is the press. Every man must lay his purse and his pen under contribution. . . . Let me pray and beseech you to set apart a certain portion of every post-day to write what may be proper for the public."

The election of 1800, the first truly national contest between organized political parties, was undoubtedly the bitterest and most slanderous in American history. Keeping with tradition, neither Federalist candidate Adams nor Republican candidate Jefferson actively campaigned. But among their followers a battle raged. In taverns and general stores, at outdoor rallies and inside halls, rival politicians exchanged words and even blows. In a not untypical Federalist slander, Jefferson was described as "nothing but a mean-spirited, low-lived fellow, the son of a half-breed Indian squaw, sired by a Virginia mulatto father, . . . raised wholly on hoe-cake, . . .bacon and hominy, with an occasional change of fricasseed bullfrog, for which abominable reptiles he had acquired a taste during his residence among the French at Paris, to whom there could be no question he would sell his country at the first offer made to him cash down, should he be elected to fill the Presidential chair." In a similar vein, the *Connecticut Courant* warned that if Jefferson won the election, "murder, rape, adultery and incest will all be openly taught and practiced."

Clearly conservative Federalists dreaded a possible Republican victory. In America of the 1790s, there had never been a peaceable transfer of power from one political party to another. Even the idea of rival parties was unacceptable; few could conceive of such a thing as a "loyal" opposition. Some Federalists, particularly in New England, viewed the world in conspiratorial terms. To them, Jefferson and the Republicans were part of a sinister plot aimed at destroying law, order, and above all Christian religion. Such people viewed the extremes of the French Revolution and the rise of the Republican Party as equal parts of an evil international conspiracy controlled and directed by a group whom they called the Bavarian Illuminati. Believers in this conspiratorial theory saw Jefferson as the chief American agent of the Illuminati.

New England clergy took the lead in the vehement denunciation of Jefferson. Dr. Timothy Dwight, the president of Yale College and a man related by blood or marriage to the political, social, and economic elite of Connecticut, frequently prophesied the dire consequences that would follow from Jefferson's election. In a Fourth of July speech, he ranted:

> For what end shall we be connected with men of whom this is the character and the conduct? . . . Is it that we may change our holy worship into a dance of Jacobin frenzy, and that we may behold a strumpet personating a goddess on the altars of Jehovah? Is it that we may see the Bible cast into a bonfire, the vessels of the sacramental supper

borne by an ass in public procession, and our children, either wheedled or terrified, uniting in chanting mockeries against God, and hailing in . . . the ruin of their religion and the loss of their souls? Is it that we may see our wives and daughters the victims of legal prostitution; soberly dishonoured; speciously polluted; the outcasts of delicacy and virtue, the loathing of God and man? . . . Shall our daughters [become] the concubines of the Illuminati?

Jefferson bore such abuse stoically, making no public effort to defend himself. Inside he fumed. Writing to a friend he admitted: "It has been a source of great pain to me to have met with so many among our opponents who had not the liberality to distinguish between political and social opposition; who transferred at once to the person the hatred they bore to his political opinions." To another friend he more candidly complained: "I have been for sometime used as the property of the newspapers, a fair mark for every man's dirt. . . . It is hard treatment, and for a singular kind of offence, that of having obtained by the labors of a life the indulgent opinions of a part of one's fellow-citizens. However, these moral evils must be submitted to like the physical scourges of tempest, fire, etc."

Despite the slander heaped upon Jefferson, his popularity and that of his party continued to grow. With an effective political organization, Republicans projected an image of the aristocratic Jefferson as "the man of the people." Their attacks on Adams and the Federalists as bent on replacing the republic with a monarchy were unfounded. Nevertheless, the real ideological differences between the parties did work in the Republicans' favor. They were after all the party of democracy and favored popular rule. Federalists, on the other hand, distrusted democracy and wished the government to remain in the hands of the rich and well born. With popular participation in elections on the rise, the Republican solicitation of the people had greater appeal than did Federalist elitism.

Republicans also benefited by a sharp rift within Federalist ranks between President Adams and followers of Hamilton. The XYZ affair and the quasi-war with France had gained the Federalists wide popular support. But in 1799, Adams had sent a peace mission to France. This time the French received the American envoys and the war scare passed. Without the patriotic unity of war and with the party in disarray, the electorate—tired of taxes, standing armies, and repressive laws—deserted the Federalists in droves.

When the electoral vote was counted, Jefferson received 73 to Adams 65. Nor did this margin of victory truly reflect the magnitude of the Republican triumph. In the congressional elections, Republicans gained an impressive 67 out of the 106 seats in the House of Representatives.

"Behold you at the head of your wise nation," Jefferson's French friend Pierre-Samuel du Pont de Nemours wrote in congratulations. "She has freely placed her greatest man in her greatest position." Celebrations, however, proved premature. Jefferson was clearly the people's choice and had won the election. Yet because under the Constitution, prior to the 12th Amendment, electors voted for two candidates rather than having separate ballots for president and vice president, Jefferson and his vice presidential running mate, Aaron Burr, ended up tied with 73 votes each. Under the Constitution the election would go to the House of Representatives for final resolution.

In the House, the lame-duck Federalist majority elected during the war crisis in 1798 plotted to overturn the popular judgment. Jefferson fretted that "after the most energetic efforts, crowned with success, we remain in the hands of our enemies." One Federalist plan called for the creation of a temporary government and another election. Other Federalists hoped to make a deal with Burr and elect him president. Even Jefferson was approached: "Many attempts have been made to obtain terms and promises from me," he divulged to Monroe. "I have declared to them unequivocally, that I would not receive the government of capitulation, that I would not go into it with my hands tied."

Dissolution of the Union or even civil war threatened. Fearing this, some moderate Federalists eventually threw their support to Jefferson. Finally, on the 36th ballot, February 17, 1801, Thomas Jefferson was elected president, marking the peaceful transfer of political power from Federalists to Republicans. Jefferson called this "the revolution of 1800" and claimed that it "was as real a revolution in the principles of our government as that of 1776 was in its form; not effected indeed by the sword, as that, but by the rational and peaceable instrument of reform, the suffrage of the people." Privilege and repression had been defeated. The future course of America would be democratic. Government henceforth would rest on the will of the people just as Jefferson had said it should some 25 years earlier in the Declaration of Independence.

7

EIGHT YEARS OF "SPLENDID MISERY"

At noon on March 4, 1801, the plainly dressed, 57-year-old Thomas Jefferson left his boarding house and walked through the muddy Washington streets to the nearby, half-completed Capitol building. There Jefferson's distant cousin and political enemy John Marshall, recently appointed by outgoing President John Adams as chief justice of the Supreme Court, administered the oath of office. In a simple service with little ceremony or pomp, Jefferson became the third president of the United States and the first inaugurated in the nation's new capital, Washington, D.C.

Yet for all its simplicity, Jefferson's inauguration was a historic event of immense importance for the young republic. A peaceable transfer of power from one political party to another had occurred, affirming the right of political opposition. Mrs. Samuel Harrison Smith, wife of the editor of the *National Intelligencer*, the capital's major newspaper, astutely observed, the inauguration was "one of the most interesting scenes a free people can ever witness. The changes of administration, which in every government and in every age have most generally been epochs of confusion, villainy and bloodshed, in this our happy country take place without any species of distraction, or disorder."

This hand-painted banner celebrates Jefferson's election victory of 1800. The eagle carries a streamer reading, "T. Jefferson, President of the United States of America. John Adams no more." (National Museum of American History, Smithsonian Institution)

Having taken the oath of office, the lanky Virginian rose to deliver his inaugural address, a speech he had labored over and one that has achieved lasting fame as a brilliant and concise proclamation of republican principles. Hoping to pacify the political passions that had so bitterly divided the nation, he called on Americans to "unite in common efforts for the common good," and to "bear in mind this sacred principle, that though the will of the majority is in all cases to prevail, that will, to be rightful, must be reasonable; that the minority possess their equal rights, which equal laws must protect, and to violate which would be oppression." He assured the people that "every difference of opinion is not a difference of principle. . . . We are all republicans—we are all federalists. If there be any among us who would wish to dissolve this Union or to change its republican form, let them stand undisturbed as monuments of the safety with which error of opinion may be tolerated where reason is left free to combat it."

His address then laid out what he deemed "the essential principles of our government." He called for "equal and exact justice to all men." In foreign affairs he pledged "peace, commerce, and honest friendship with all nations, entangling alliances with none." The sum of good government, he concluded, was to be "wise and frugal," to "restrain men from injuring one another," to "leave them otherwise free to regulate their own pursuits of industry and improvement," and "not take from the mouth of labor the bread it has earned." Calling for "freedom of religion; freedom of the press; freedom of person under the protection of the *habeas corpus* [the prohibition of imprisonment without charge]; and trial by juries impartially selected—these principles form the bright constellation which has gone before us, and guided our steps through an age of revolution and reformation. . . . They should be the creed of our political faith, the text of civic instruction, the touchstone by which we try the services of those we trust."

From the outset of his presidency, Jefferson sought to create an air of republican simplicity in contrast to the formal and regal ceremony with which the Federalists had surrounded the presidency. Unlike his predecessors, Washington and Adams, he refused to hold stuffy receptions. When Anthony Merry, the newly appointed British minister, arrived at the executive mansion to present his credentials, he was shocked to encounter Jefferson wearing casual dress and in his bedroom slippers. The president cancelled the state carriage with its six horses and liveried servants, choosing instead to ride about on horseback unattended.

A generous host, President Jefferson held frequent dinner parties. Here too informality reigned. As Ambassador Merry noted, "When brought together in society, all are perfectly equal, whether foreign or domestic, titled or untitled, in or out of office." Jefferson had a round dining table and seated his guests indiscriminately with no designated place of honor.

Yet as an astute politician, Jefferson's dinner parties were more than displays of democratic manners. At least three times a week, the president invited members of Congress in groups of about 12 at a time. In addition to being *the* social events in the sparsely populated new capital, Jefferson's dinners furthered his political purposes. As he explained it:

> I cultivate personal intercourse with the legislature that we may know one another and have opportunities of little explanations of circumstances, which, not understood, might produce jealousies and suspicions injurious to the public interest, which is best promoted by harmony and mutual confidence among its functionaries. I depend much on the members for the local information necessary in local matters, as well as for the means of getting at public sentiment.

New York Congressman Samuel Mitchill described Jefferson's dinners as "easy and sociable." The president's French chef, Mitchill noted, "understands the art of preparing and serving up food, to a nicety." A dessert of ice cream baked in pastry particularly impressed the congressman. Jefferson himself ordered his fine French wines at a price of nearly $2,800 annually. Indeed Jefferson's yearly household expenditures exceeded his $25,000 presidential salary by more than $8,500 and left him further in debt. But his dinners served Jefferson's political purposes well. Seldom if ever has a president enjoyed a closer working relationship with Congress. Virtually all of his desired policies were enacted into law.

Affable entertainments were only one reason for Jefferson's effectiveness as a political leader. He also worked extremely hard in office. As was his habit of a lifetime, Jefferson rose regularly at five in the morning and read and wrote until about nine. He spent the next few hours consulting with members of his cabinet and other government officials. He relied particularly on his secretary of state, James Madison, and his secretary of the treasury, Albert Gallatin. In the early afternoon, the president generally took a horseback ride, which gave him exercise and allowed him time to reflect on matters of state. His dinners commenced at three-thirty, although occasionally a guest would be invited earlier for a private predinner consultation. Punctually at six in the evening, Jefferson would return to his study and remain at his desk until retiring at ten.

The first term of this hardworking president proved a great success. Jefferson set out to reverse what he saw as more than a decade of Federalist abuses of power. He allowed the hated Alien and Sedition Acts to expire and pardoned those still in jail under the Sedition Act. In 1802, Congress, at Jefferson's behest, liberalized the naturalization law, allowing immigrants to become full citizens after only five years of residence rather than fourteen. That same year, Jefferson succeeded in getting Congress to repeal most internal taxes, including the detested whiskey tax. To offset the reduced revenues and root out what he saw as the Federalists' "dissipation of treasure," Jefferson drastically slashed federal expenditures. He fired tax collectors, simplified the court system, cut the military budget in half, and closed several embassies abroad. These reduced expenditures, combined with swelling tariff revenues because of expanding trade, allowed Jefferson and treasury secretary Gallatin to greatly reduce the national debt. While Hamilton and the Federalists had viewed a permanent federal debt as a way of strengthening the government by throwing the support of the rich behind it, to Jefferson the debt was a source of "corruption and rottenness." By the time he retired from office in 1809, the $80 million federal debt that his administration had inherited had been reduced by nearly half.

Jefferson's policies of reform and conciliation did much to restore the political peace after a decade of partisan strife. The president was proud that "without a direct tax, without internal taxes, and without borrowing" his government was making great strides to pay off the public debt and emancipate "our posterity from that moral canker." The country prospered and people were content. Jefferson had reason to believe that "by a steady pursuit of economy and peace, and by the establishment of Republican principles in substance and in form" that Federalism would sink "into an abyss from which there shall be no resurrection for it." The Revolution, Jefferson believed, was finally fulfilled:

> Our people in a body are wise, because they are under the unrestrained and unperverted operation of their own understanding. . . . A nation composed of such materials, and free in all its members from distressing wants, furnishes hopeful implements for the interesting experiment of self-government; and we feel that we are acting under obligations not confined to the limits of our own society. It is impossible not to be sensible that we are acting for all mankind.

However, this tranquility was quickly checked by momentous news that threatened the very existence of the American experiment. Soon after coming to the presidency, Jefferson heard rumors that Spain had secretly ceded to France the port of New Orleans and the vast Louisiana Territory stretching from the Mississippi to the Rockies. Dependent on the Mississippi River for access to world markets and envisioning that one day the boundaries of the United States would span the continent, Jefferson took alarm. While the Spanish presence had always appeared as an impediment to American ambitions, Spain was weak and posed no real threat. France, on the other hand, had emerged under Napoleon Bonaparte as the most powerful and aggressive nation in Europe. Should France occupy New Orleans, this would force Americans, warned Jefferson, to "marry ourselves to the British fleet and nation."

The marriage proved unnecessary. In 1802, Napoleon sent some 30,000 of his best troops to possess the Louisiana Territory, ordering them first to stop in Santo Domingo and suppress a slave insurrection that had been raging on that Caribbean island for several years. These crack French forces got no further. Guerrilla fighters and yellow fever devastated Napoleon's army and dashed his hopes of recreating a French empire in the New World. When Jefferson's special emissary James Monroe arrived in France in April 1803 with orders to try to purchase the port of New Orleans, he was astounded to find the French offering to sell all of the Louisiana Territory to the United States for a price of $15 million. Monroe quickly agreed, and a treaty was signed on May 2.

News of the treaty reached Washington on July 3, 1803. The following day, the *National Intelligencer* announced that the Fourth of July was "a proud day for the President" who had earned "the widespread joy of millions at an event which history will record among the most splendid in our annals." At a cost of less than four cents an acre the United States had acquired a magnificent wilderness empire that doubled the nation's size, safeguarded the Mississippi, eliminated European threats, and assured the country's future greatness as a continental power. This, boasted Jefferson, "secures to us the course of a peaceable nation." Calling the new lands an "empire of liberty," he told Congress that the acquisition offered "an ample provision for our posterity, and a widespread field for the blessings of freedom and equal laws."

Although overwhelmingly popular, the Louisiana Purchase posed constitutional problems. The Constitution made no provision for buying foreign territory. This bothered Jefferson. In his attacks on the Bank of the United States, the Alien and Sedition Acts, and other Federalist legislation, he had always insisted on a strict construction of the Constitution, limiting federal powers to those explicitly set forth. Wishing to avoid violating the letter of the Constitution, Jefferson drafted an amendment to legalize the purchase. But under pressure from his cabinet and congressional Republicans to act fast lest Napoleon find some pretext to withdraw his remarkable offer, Jefferson swallowed his constitutional scruples and the Senate quickly ratified the treaty.

Even before the surprising French offer, Jefferson's fascination with the uncharted lands west of the Mississippi led him to secretly arrange an exploratory party. To head this expedition the president chose his Virginia neighbor and private secretary, Meriwether Lewis. Although only 28, Lewis, an army captain, already had some knowledge of the western country. Lewis in turn picked as his second in command William Clark, younger brother of Revolutionary War hero George Rogers Clark.

Lewis and Clark with a party of about 25 others set forth from St. Louis in May 1804. Their official instructions were to trace the Missouri River to its source, cross the western mountains, and follow the best water route to the Pacific. Jefferson explained to Congress that the object was to find "the most direct and practicable water communication across this continent, for the purposes of commerce." But Jefferson's chief concern was the advancement of scientific knowledge. His private instructions to Lewis asked him to obtain accurate measurements of latitude and longitude; to compile data on Indian tribes, their languages and customs; and to gather information on climate, plants, mammals, reptiles, insects, rocks, soils, and volcanoes. Jefferson even sent Lewis to the American Philosophical Society in Philadelphia for a cram course in zoology, astronomy, and botany prior to his departure.

The results of Lewis and Clark's incredible two-year adventure did not disappoint. Although failing to find the impossible—a direct water link to the Pacific—they cataloged a dazzling array of new plants and animals, including vast herds of buffalo, elk, and antelope; made contact with more than 50 Indian tribes; crossed the treacherous Rockies; paddled down the Columbia River to the Pacific; and retraversed the continent. Their priceless scientific and geographic information and their glowing descriptions of the vast new territory fueled the popular imagination and helped stimulate westward migration.

By the time Jefferson stood for reelection in the fall of 1804, peace, prosperity, and the exhilaration of the Louisiana Purchase made him unquestionably the most popular person in America. In the election, the dispirited Federalists suffered disastrous defeat. Their presidential candidate, Charles C. Pinckney, carried only Connecticut and Delaware and lost to Jefferson in the electoral college by an overwhelming vote of 162 to 14. In Congress, as well, Republican candidates gained substantially. Basking in the sun of success with the Federalist Party seemingly eliminated as a force in national politics, Jefferson and the Republicans looked forward to four more tranquil years.

Events abroad, however, quickly dashed these hopes. Rivalry between Britain and France had made possible the acquisition of Louisiana during Jefferson's first term. European fighting intensified during his second administration. Crowned emperor of the French in 1804, Napoleon set out to conquer Europe. To counter this, Britain, allied with Austria, Russia, and Sweden, doggedly fought the ambitious emperor. In the struggle that followed, the United States tried to remain neutral but soon found itself a pawn in an international chess game over which it had little control. As a result, Jefferson's second term would prove as frustrating as his first had been fulfilling.

In October 1805, British Admiral Horatio Nelson won a smashing victory over the combined French and Spanish fleets in the Battle of Trafalgar. This left Britain the supreme power on the high seas. Less than two months later, Napoleon won a decisive victory at Austerlitz that demolished the British coalition. "What an awful spectacle does the world exhibit at this instant," Jefferson anguished in January 1806, "one man bestriding the continent of Europe like a Colossus, and another roaming unbridled on the ocean."

With Britain unable to mount a successful campaign against the French armies and Napoleon's navy powerless against the English fleet, both belligerents turned to economic warfare. Britain declared a blockade of the European continent, and beginning in 1805, the Royal Navy contemptuously stopped American ships, searched them, and confiscated those carrying goods to or from Britain's enemies. In response, Napoleon authorized the seizure of neutral vessels that had undergone a British search or called at a British port. From the 1790s through 1805, the American merchant marine had experienced meteoric growth and fantastic profits. But now, as the premier neutral shipping nation, the United States found itself caught in a bind and watched helplessly as the two superpowers captured its ships.

Although Britain and France both violated America's neutral rights, the former mother country came in for more blame. Not only did the Royal Navy snatch more U.S. merchant vessels than the French, they also impressed (drafted into their own naval forces) American seamen.

British warships had reputations as "floating hells." Discipline was harsh and wages wretched. As a result, whenever a British man-o'-war docked at a foreign port, a fair number of the crew jumped ship. Many of these deserters did end up in the American merchant service where pay was higher and working conditions better. To retrieve these men the British adapted the practice of boarding American vessels and impressing anyone they deemed to be English into service in the Royal Navy. While many thus impressed were British deserters, thousands were naturalized Americans or even native-born citizens. Such a policy violated American sovereignty and injured the nation's pride.

American indignation at British arrogance erupted into war frenzy in June 1807, when the British warship *Leopard* opened fire on the USS *Chesapeake*, killing or wounding 21 men and seizing four alleged deserters. "Never since the battle of Lexington," claimed Jefferson, "have I seen this country in such a state of exasperation as at present."

While war awaited only Jefferson's word, the president sought peace. At first, he attempted through negotiations with

Britain to gain redress for the *Chesapeake* atrocity. When this came to naught, he plotted a bold policy of commercial retaliation. In December 1807, he steered the Embargo Act through Congress. The law prohibited American vessels from sailing to foreign ports and forbade foreign vessels from taking on cargoes in the United States. Jefferson's hope was that "having taught so many other useful lessons to Europe" America might now show them "that there are peaceable means of repressing injustice, by making it the interest of the aggressor to do what is just, and abstain from future wrong." The embargo began with substantial public support. Jefferson optimistically believed that by isolating the United States from "the present paroxysm of the insanity of Europe" war could be avoided.

Unfortunately this well-intentioned experiment in using what Jefferson termed "peaceable coercion" as an alternative to war wreaked havoc on the American economy and soon became highly unpopular. The northern ports, particularly in New England, suffered severely. Thousands of seamen found themselves out of work; merchants were driven into debt or bankruptcy; farmers with international markets closed were devastated. Southern planters, too, including Jefferson, lost much financially. Opposition to the embargo led to a revival of the Federalist Party. Some New England politicians even talked openly of secession. Smuggling became widespread.

The failure of the embargo to win concessions from either Britain or France combined with the swelling domestic opposition to the act finally forced Jefferson to modify his policy. On March 1, 1809, in his last act as president, he signed the Non-Intercourse Act, which replaced the embargo. This measure opened trade to all nations except Britain and France and provided that if either belligerent revoked its restrictions on neutral shipping, then nonintercourse would be maintained only against the other.

Jefferson had overestimated European dependence on American trade. His successor, James Madison, would continue efforts to manipulate the great powers through economic coercion, but he would also fail to change their behavior. Ultimately in 1812, the United States declared war on Great Britain. Yet while the embargo proved a flawed policy, its results were not all bad. The embargo bought the United States time that allowed the nation to prepare for war. It also encouraged domestic manufactures and therefore lessened American dependence on Europe. When war ultimately did come, the United States prevailed. And by war's end in 1815, America had succeeded in isolating itself from the jaws of European imperial ambitions. By then the nation stood on the threshold of an era of vast economic and geographical expansion. Jefferson's aspirations would be fulfilled.

While the embargo clouded Jefferson's last year in office, his personal popularity remained high. Had he chosen, he certainly could have won reelection for a third term. As it was, he chose to follow the precedent of Washington and step down after two terms. He did have the pleasure of seeing his closest friend James Madison easily elected to succeed him. Reflecting on Jefferson's eight years in the highest office, Congressman John Rhea proclaimed: "During that term of time the United States (certain disagreeable occurrences arising from exterior relations notwithstanding) have been in possession of national happiness and prosperity, unexampled in the annals of nations." Jefferson, he concluded, had created "a government founded on reason. . . . To make the people of the United States respectable, happy, great and independent as possible, was the object of the administration of Mr. Jefferson."

Jefferson stood rightly proud of his accomplishments. But by 1809, having served his country for some 40 years, he yearned to retire to the tranquility of Monticello and to his family, his books, and his farms. A few days before leaving office he confessed, "Never did a prisoner, released from his chains, feel such relief as I shall on shaking off the shackles of power." In a letter to a friend he wrote: "Nature intended me for the tranquil pursuits of science, by rendering them my supreme delight. But the enormities of the times in which I have lived have forced me to take a part in resisting them, and to commit myself on the boisterous ocean of political passions." Free at last from his "eight years of splendid misery," Jefferson bid farewell to Washington friends and returned to his beloved mountaintop.

8

"ARCHITECTURE IS MY DELIGHT"

T homas Jefferson was a man of remarkably diverse talents. However, outside the realm of politics, his most enduring and creative contributions came in the field of architecture. While still a student at the College of William and Mary, he acquired his first book on architecture from an old cabinetmaker. From that day forward, architecture became one of the great passions of his life. As he later confessed: "Architecture is my delight, and putting up and pulling down, one of my favorite amusements." By the time of his death in 1826, he had designed some of the country's most significant public and private buildings. Without doubt, he was the most important American architect of his time.

Professionally trained architects were rare in colonial America. Skilled carpenter-craftsmen produced most buildings, generally with the guidance of English pattern books. Today many people admire the remaining 18th-century structures. Indeed, the restored colonial Williamsburg, Jefferson's college town, has become a major tourist attraction.

To Jefferson, however, few buildings in that town or the surrounding countryside warranted admiration. He described William and Mary's edifices and the nearby hospital as "rude, mis-shapen piles, which, but that they have roofs, would be taken for brick-kilns." Speaking more generally he lamented:

> The genius of architecture seems to have shed its maledic-
> tions over this land. Buildings are often erected, by
> individuals, of considerable expense. To give these symme-
> try and taste, would not increase their cost. It would only
> change the arrangement of the materials, the form and
> combination of the members. This would often cost less
> than the burthen of barbarous ornaments with which
> these buildings are sometimes charged. But the first prin-
> ciples of the art are unknown, and there exists scarcely a
> model among us sufficiently chaste to give an idea of them.

One problem, as Jefferson saw it, was that "private buildings
are very rarely constructed of stone or brick, much the greatest
portion being of . . . boards plastered with lime. It is impossible
to devise things more ugly, uncomfortable, and happily more
perishable." Even "the poorest people's" crude log huts he found
preferable to the wood-framed houses of the rich. "A country
whose buildings are of wood," he concluded, "can never increase
in its improvements to any considerable degree. Their duration
is highly estimated at fifty years. Every half century
then . . . we have to set out anew. . . . Whereas when buildings
are of durable materials, every new edifice is an actual and
permanent acquisition to the State, adding to its value as well
as to its ornament."

Wood fabrication, however, was only part of the problem. A
more serious error from Jefferson's perspective was that most
American constructions derived from English customs and
designs. Just as in politics, America needed an architecture
independent from Great Britain and worthy of the new republic. The object of properly constructed buildings, claimed
Jefferson, "is to improve the taste of my countrymen, to increase their reputation, and to reconcile to them the respect of
the world and procure them its praise." In a letter to his friend
James Madison he asked: "How is a taste in this beautiful art
to be formed in our countrymen unless we avail ourselves of
every occasion when public buildings are to be erected, of
presenting to them models for their study and imitation."

Although he personally appreciated fine painting and
sculpture, Jefferson judged these arts as "too expensive for
the state of wealth among us." Architecture on the other
hand was both the most visible and the most practical of the
arts and therefore "worth great attention." "As we double our

numbers every 20 years we must double our houses," asserted Jefferson, "and it is desirable to introduce taste into an art which shows so much."

But where was America to turn for architectural models? The desire for cultural as well as political independence meant rejecting British designs. Nor was France much help; the excessively ornate rococo style current there during Jefferson's stay he deemed "far from chaste." Furthermore most of the great works of European architecture aggrandized and amplified the authority of the church and of kings, queens, and the nobility. What America needed was an architecture that would extol the sovereignty of the people. Jefferson found his model in the classical architecture of ancient Rome.

At about the time he wrote the Declaration of Independence, Jefferson first proposed using a Roman temple as a model for the Governor's Palace in Williamsburg. Although this plan was never implemented, Jefferson retained the idea of employing Roman models to express the greatness of the American republic. Here was an architecture that was monumental and dignified without being overly adorned. While borrowing the use of Ionic, Doric, and Corinthian capitals and columns from the Greeks, the Romans had perfected the arch, the vault, and the dome—all of which Jefferson would employ. This gave Roman architecture unlimited prospects of design and application.

Jefferson also was drawn to Roman architecture because it confirmed his enlightened world view. Classical architecture appeared lawful and reasonable. Its functional contrasts of vertical supports and horizontal loads conformed to mathematically defined proportions. Here was an architecture that gave visible testament to his Newtonian faith in the laws of nature. Aesthetically Roman architecture, from Jefferson's perspective, reflected humanity's innate love of order in this rational and harmonious universe.

As with so many things, Jefferson first encountered Roman buildings through books. After initially reading texts by such notable English architects as James Gibbs and Robert Morris, Jefferson discovered the four-volume study of Roman buildings by the 16th-century Italian Andrea Palladio. Virtually unknown in America at that time, Palladio had made an intensive investigation of surviving Roman structures. He also had compiled information drawn from ancient writers on Roman country villas that no longer existed. Palladio laid out exacting rules of proportions that appealed to Jefferson's mathematical mind.

Yet while Roman architecture in general and Palladio in particular would strongly influence Jefferson, his own designs were never just copies. As an architect, he freely adapted Palladian and Roman models to fit the American environment and the needs of the new nation. He built with native materials and frequently made innovations and improvements. The resulting creations are uniquely Jeffersonian and anything but mechanical reproductions of classical buildings. This can be seen in examining his most famous designs—his house Monticello, the Virginia State Capitol at Richmond, and the University of Virginia at Charlottesville.

Monticello, Jefferson's mountaintop home, was a labor of love that lasted nearly a lifetime. Jefferson was both architect and builder, and the house changed and grew as he matured. The first working drawings he made date from 1767 when he was 24. Construction began in 1769, and by November 1770 a small building that today flanks the south side of the main house was complete enough for Jefferson to move in.

Jefferson's general design derived partly from Palladio in its arrangement of a central living section with projecting wings running east and west. Palladio had written that one should "build upon elevated and cheerful places, where the air is, by the continual blowing of the winds, moved; and the earth, by its declivity, purged of all ill vapours and moisture; and where the inhabitants are healthy and cheerful, and preserve a good colour." Whether this influenced Jefferson in choosing his mountain site is not known, but certainly he loved his hilltop setting. He wrote:

> And our own dear Monticello, where has nature spread so rich a mantle under the eye? mountains, forests, rocks, rivers. With what majesty do we there ride above the storms! how sublime to look down into the workhouse of nature, to see here clouds, hail, snow, rain, thunder, all fabricated at our feet! And the glorious Sun, when rising as if out of a distant water, just gilding the tops of the mountains, and giving life to all nature!

One uniquely Jeffersonian innovation was the placement of the "dependencies"—kitchen, dairy, smokehouse, ice house, servants' quarters, laundry room, carriage garage, and horse stalls. Unlike other Virginia plantations where such necessities filled the grounds with various outbuildings, at Monticello they were grouped below the main house, opening on one side to ground level but otherwise covered with terraces so as to be invisible from the lawns, entrances, and first floor because of the slope of the hilltop. Thus visitors to Monticello seldom saw slaves, servants, or workplaces.

By the early 1780s, Jefferson's first version of Monticello was nearly complete. The Chevalier de Chastellux, visiting Jefferson in 1782, left this description:

> This house, of which Mr. Jefferson was the architect, and often the builder, is constructed in an Italian style, and is quite tasteful. . . . It consists of a large square pavilion, into which one enters through two porticoes ornamented with columns. The ground floor consists chiefly of a large and lofty *salon*, or drawing room, which is to be decorated entirely in the antique style; above the *salon* is a library of the same form; two small wings, with only a ground floor and attic, are joined to this pavilion, and are intended to communicate with the kitchen, offices, etc., which will form on either side a kind of basement topped by a terrace. My object in giving these details is not to describe the house, but to prove that it resembles none of the others seen in this country; so that it may be said that Mr. Jefferson is the first American who has consulted the Fine Arts to know how he should shelter himself from the weather.

The years from 1784 to 1789 that Jefferson served as ambassador to France gave him his first direct experience of classical and contemporary European architecture. He was enthralled and confessed to having gazed upon the exquisite Roman temple, the Maison Carrée at Nîmes, "like a lover at his mistress." Throughout his years abroad he devoted much time to the study of ancient and modern buildings. He had a craftsman's feeling for materials and workmanship. On a tour of the French region of Bordeaux, for instance, he carefully measured the bricks of an ancient Roman circus (arena), describing their texture as "compact, and solid as that of porcelain."

While residing in Paris in 1785, Jefferson received a letter from his friend Madison informing him that the Virginia Assembly had commissioned him to find a French architect to draw up plans for the new state capitol at Richmond. Although consulting with French architect Charles-Louis Clerisseau, noted for his studies of Roman antiquities, Jefferson himself made the design based on the Maison Carrée that he considered "the most perfect model existing." Sending his plans to Virginia, he described the proposed building as "simple and sublime. More cannot be said. They are not the brat of a chimerical [imaginary] conception never before brought to light, but copied from the most perfect model of ancient architecture remaining on earth; one which has received the approbation [praise] of near 2,000 years and which is sufficiently remarkable to have been visited by all travelers."

Again Jefferson's design was no mere reproduction. To adapt the Roman temple to serve as a modern state capitol, Jefferson substituted windows for the pilasters of the outer walls; one of the three rows of columns was dropped from the portico to admit more light; to suit the simple values of a republic, all statuary was eliminated from the exterior; and crowning the columns that held the front portico, the simpler Ionic capitals replaced the more ornate Corinthian capitals of the original. Jefferson also drew a plan for the interior with rooms suitable for the separate legislative, executive, and judicial branches of government.

When finally completed, the Capitol at Richmond stood as an elegant architectural statement of republican ideals. A touring Frenchman, François de La Rochefoucauld-Liancourt, pronounced the building "beyond comparison the most beautiful, the most noble, and the greatest in all America." As the first modern adaptation of a Roman temple for a large public building, the Virginia Capitol would stimulate a classical revival, not merely in America, but in Europe as well.

Upon his return to the United States late in 1789, Jefferson was quickly thrust into the fury of American politics. But in 1794, soon after resigning his post as secretary of state, he set himself the momentous task of completely rebuilding his revered Monticello. Over the next decade and a half, the house

Thomas Jefferson's Virginia State Capitol at Richmond (Author's collection)

was transformed into the magnificent mansion that we know today. Influenced now both by classical design and the lovely one-story villas he had seen in Paris, Jefferson doubled the size of the house and added a dome modeled on the Halle aux Bleds in Paris. The new design hid the second story, which could be reached by narrow, private stairways.

Jefferson paid close attention to detail. He established a brick kiln on the property, a nail factory, and a sawmill so that most construction materials could be produced on the site. Other items such as windows, marble, silks, and furnishing he imported at great expense from Europe. He even made sketches for the color and design of curtains and wallpapers. The finished house was an elegant 35-room mansion. Entering by the east portico, visitors would have noticed a weather vane on the roof. This was ingeniously connected to a compass arrow on the inside ceiling of the portico so that one could read the wind direction without going outside. Other Jeffersonian innovations and inventions included a seven-day clock operated by weights that descended into the basement; a pair of glass doors that both opened when one was lightly touched; dumbwaiters in the dining room to give easy access to the kitchen and wine cellar below; numerous skylights and air shafts for light and ventilation; toilets connected to small tunnels for carrying away waste; fireplaces with cast-iron panels on the back and sides to radiate heat more efficiently; and a swivel chair of his own invention in his study.

Observing Jefferson's house while still under construction in 1796, La Rochefoucauld-Liancourt noted that

> Monticello, according to the first plan, was infinitely superior to all other houses in America, in point of taste and convenience; but at that time Mr. Jefferson had studied taste and fine arts in books only. His travels in Europe have supplied him with models; he has appropriated them to his design; and his new plan, the execution of which is already much advanced, will be accomplished before the end of next year, and then his house will certainly deserve to be ranked with the most pleasant mansions in France and England.

The Frenchman was right about the excellence of the house, but overly optimistic as to its completion date. Jefferson's return to public life—first as vice president and then as president—delayed matters. Not until 1809 would Monticello in its present form be substantially finished. During these years, Jefferson also worked on aesthetically improving Monticello's grounds, creating one of the first and certainly one of the finest landscaped gardens in America. Shunning the formal gardens of the French, Jefferson used the more wild, natural, and romantic English gardens as his model and admirably adapted this style to fit the environment and the abundant plant life of his native Virginia. One recent scholar has credited Jefferson with "laying the foundation for . . . the profession of *landscape architecture*."

Jefferson also found time during this busy period of his life to design houses for a number of friends, including future presidents Madison and James Monroe as well as his daughter Martha. He also drew plans for a prison, a church, two county courthouses and several other public buildings in Virginia. Additionally, Jefferson played a major role in the design and layout of Washington, D.C.

In 1806, even before completing Monticello, Jefferson started work on Poplar Forest, his country retreat some 90 miles from his more famous estate. Scholars today consider Poplar Forest "one of Jefferson's most remarkable architectural achievements" and also one of his "most original." An eight-sided structure—the first octagonal building in America—the house has a tall square dining room in the center lighted by skylights and surrounded by a series of octagonal rooms. Even the terraces around the house are octagons. In his later years, Jefferson loved to spend time at Poplar Forest.

The crowning achievement of Jefferson's architectural career came late in his life when he designed the University of Virginia. Midway through his presidency, Jefferson had outlined a plan for a state-supported university. It was to be an institution, in his words, "based on the ultimate freedom of the human mind" (see chapter 10). He also conceived of it as "an academical village rather than of one large building." In 1810, he expressed this then-unique idea more precisely as "a small and separate lodge for each separate professorship, with only

The west front of Monticello as depicted by artist George Cooke (Family Magazine, Vol. IV, 1837)

a hall below for his class, and two chambers above for himself; joining the lodges by barracks for a certain portion of students, opening into a covered way to give a dry communication between all the schools. The whole of these arranged around an open square of grass and trees."

Not until 1817 did Jefferson's plan win approval for building the university at Charlottesville, not far from Monticello. Jefferson visited the site that summer and marked the locations for the buildings. On October 6, 1817, with President Monroe officiating and former presidents Jefferson and Madison assisting, the cornerstone for the first of what would be 10 pavilion lodges was laid. The 74-year-old Jefferson designed all the buildings and supervised construction. Work continued for several years. In 1822, a visitor from Vermont reported seeing the then 79-year-old Jefferson take a chisel from the hand of an Italian stonecutter to show him how to cut the spiral scroll of an Ionic capital.

Jefferson's design was a quadrangle, open at the south end, with the pavilion lodges for classrooms, professors' lodgings, and student dormitories lining each side and leading up to a great Rotunda at the north end. Although all the pavilions were based on classical designs, they were each unique with their capitals representing the three Greek orders—Doric, Ionic, and Corinthian. Jefferson's hope was that they would serve as "models of taste and correct architecture" and "as specimens of orders for the architectural lectures." From north to south the lodges were made increasingly longer. Thus, looking down the quadrangle from in front of the Rotunda they present the illusion of being of equal size.

The focal point of Jefferson's grand design was the Rotunda. Inspired by Palladio's drawings of the Roman Pantheon, the Rotunda was mathematically proportioned so that the horizontal and vertical lines of the building exactly squared a circle formed by the dome. The beautiful dome, neither heavy nor obtrusive, crowns the building. Inside, the lower floor, according to Jefferson, had "large rooms for religious worship, for public examinations, and other associated purposes. The upper floor is a single room for a Library, canopied by the Dome and its skylight."

Visitors particularly admired the vastness and beauty of the library. It was lined with 40 polished columns of Italian

The University of Virginia as depicted in an 1827 engraving by B. Tanner
(The Betts Collection, Alderman Library, University of Virginia)

Carrara marble with Corinthian capitals supporting an elegant circular entablature. Near the top of the columns, a balustraded balcony encircled the room. Above was the lofty dome and its bright skylight.

The diverse buildings of the university unite in a harmonious architectural masterpiece. The pavilions, beautifully proportioned variations of classical design, lead up a series of terraces to the great Rotunda with its sparkling white dome—the capstone of Jefferson's creation. George Ticknor, a brilliant young Harvard professor, gazing on the nearly completed buildings in 1824, pronounced them "more beautiful than anything architectural in New England, and more appropriate to a university than is to be found, perhaps, in the world." Indeed, in celebrating the nation's bicentennial in 1976, the American Institute of Architects named Jefferson's buildings at the University of Virginia as the finest complex erected in the United States since 1776.

Masterpieces such as the University of Virginia, the Virginia Capitol, and Monticello would stand out as architectural gems in any age. Although not professionally trained, Thomas Jefferson was certainly a true architect in the modern sense. He made preliminary studies, working plans, and full-scale drawings of details. He specified site locations and materials, and he supervised construction. His influence has been immense. Today, nearly all of the nation's 50 state capitols are variations of Jeffersonian buildings, and numerous universities and other public buildings have made use of Jeffersonian designs as well.

Jefferson's long and remarkable service to his country as political theorist, statesman, ambassador, and elected official has long overshadowed his proficiency as an architect. Yet it is fair to say that even if he had never held political office he would still be remembered as the foremost architect of his age.

9

SLAVERY: "THE WOLF BY THE EARS"

homas Jefferson's earliest childhood memory was of being carried on a cushion held by a slave on horseback riding some 70 miles from his home at Shadwell to his temporary home at Tuckahoe. He grew up on plantations surrounded by slaves. At the time he wrote the Declaration of Independence, he owned about 200 slaves. Monticello itself was largely built by slave labor, and the sumptuous life that he enjoyed there depended on the profits he made from slavery. Slaves cooked his meals and tilled his fields. Even as president, he bought and sold slaves. When he died in 1826, a slave carpenter crafted his coffin. In his will he freed only five of the more than 200 slaves that he owned. Soon after his death, his grandson and executor, Thomas Jefferson Randolph, found it necessary to auction some "130 valuable negroes" because of the very large debt Jefferson had left.

Yet despite the fact that throughout his life Jefferson was entangled with slavery, he genuinely hated human bondage and looked forward to the day when this curse could be forever eradicated from the land. He wrote: "The love of justice and the love of country plead equally the cause of these people, and it is a moral reproach to us that they should have pleaded it so long in vain." As an enlightened intellectual, Jefferson denounced slavery as a "hideous evil" and a violation of the most basic human rights.

From early on in his public career, Jefferson attempted to reform the slave system. When first elected to the House of Burgesses in 1769, he sought to make it legal for slave owners to free their slaves. His fellow legislators rejected this measure. A year later, the young lawyer took free of charge the case of a black slave suing for his freedom. In his plea, Jefferson argued that "under the law of nature, all men are born free, and every one comes into the world with a right to his own person, which includes the liberty of moving and using it at his own will." Again his efforts came to naught.

Jefferson's powerful 1774 pamphlet, *A Summary View of the Rights of British America* (see chapter 2), claimed that the abolition of slavery was "the great object of desire in these colonies" and blamed King George III for perpetuating the "detestable" institution. He continued this line of argument in his rough draft of the Declaration of Independence, asserting that the king had "waged cruel war against human nature itself, violating the most sacred right of life and liberty in the persons of a distant people who never offended him, captivating and carrying them into slavery in another hemisphere, or to incur miserable death in their transportation thither."

Although the facts show Jefferson's charge a gross exaggeration, nevertheless, he truly believed that once Americans overthrew the cruel oppression of George III, the slave trade would be abolished and slavery itself would soon wither away. Jefferson was the first eminent American statesman publicly to denounce slavery as a crime against human nature and against the fundamental rights for which the Revolution was being waged. Congress's deletion of his paragraph on slavery left him distraught (see chapter 1).

Yet even without Jefferson's specific attack on slavery, the Declaration of Independence in its final form greatly furthered the antislavery cause. By asserting that "*all* men are created equal" and "endowed by their Creator" with "unalienable rights" to "life, liberty and the pursuit of happiness," Jefferson unequivocally denied the right of one person to own another. Prior to 1776, opponents of slavery were few and ineffective. After the adoption of the Declaration, however, numerous antislavery societies sprang up, and over the next two decades every northern state made provisions to abolish slavery. In many of the court cases and legislative decisions that accomplished this, abolitionists directly cited the Declaration. Thus, in no small measure due to Jefferson, by the end of the 18th century, slavery, which had existed throughout America, had been contained within the southern states.

Soon after drafting the Declaration of Independence, Jefferson drew up a constitution for Virginia that provided for the gradual emancipationof slaves. This plan was rejected, but in 1783, Jefferson presented a similar proposal stipulating that all children born of slave parents after 1800 were to be free on reaching adulthood. The legislature rebuffed this scheme as well.

Failing in Virginia, Jefferson turned his attention to preventing the spread of slavery into the western territories. In 1784, he proposed a congressional ordinance declaring slavery illegal in all western territories after the year 1800. The northern states supported him on this, but most southern delegates, including the other members of the Virginia delegation, opposed it. When the vote came, six states favored the measure, six opposed. John Beatty of New Jersey, who backed Jefferson's plan, lay sick in bed and did not attend the session. The tie effectively defeated the measure. Three years later, the Northwest Ordinance banned slavery north of the Ohio River, but not to the south. Jefferson lamented the loss of this opportunity to stop the spread of slavery. To a French friend he wrote dejectedly: "The voice of a single individual would have prevented this abominable crime from spreading itself over the new country. Thus we see the fate of millions unborn hanging on the tongue of one man, and Heaven was silent in that awful moment!"

The failure to achieve an end to slavery in his native Virginia or in the western territories south of the Ohio seems to have cooled Jefferson's ardor for the cause of antislavery. In his two terms as president, only on one occasion did he speak out on this issue. In his annual message to Congress in December 1806, he urged legislation to abolish the African slave trade that he had first attacked in his *Summary View*. When the Constitution had been drawn up in 1787, as a concession to the lower south, a compromise was adopted prohibiting Congress from abolishing the slave trade prior to 1808. More than a year before the deadline Jefferson beseeched Congress to take action:

> I congratulate you, fellow-citizens, on the approach of the period at which you may interpose your authority constitutionally, to withdraw the citizens of the United states from all further participation in those violations of human rights, which have been so long continued on the unoffending inhabitants of Africa, and which the morality, the reputation, and the best interests of our country have long been eager to proscribe.

Congress quickly passed a law prohibiting the further import of slaves from Africa as of January 1, 1808. Jefferson may have thought that this was enough and that without the importation of additional slaves the institution would gradually wane. Unfortunately, however, a high slave birthrate coupled with the great demand for slave labor with the spread of cotton plantations through the deep South witnessed a vast increase in the slave population and its economic importance.

On retiring from public life Jefferson grew increasingly apathetic about slavery. In 1814, Edward Coles, a young neighbor and disciple of Jefferson's, wrote to the former president asking for his support in the campaign against slavery. Coles urged the elder statesman "to put into complete practice those hallowed principles contained in that renowned Declaration, of which you were the immortal author." Jefferson counseled Coles to work "softly but steadily" for emancipation and promised to give the cause "all my prayers, and these are the only weapons of an old man." But when Coles proposed moving with his own slaves to Illinois and setting them free, Jefferson advised only gradual emancipation. People "of this color," he wrote, were "as incapable as children of taking care of themselves." Free blacks, he added, were "pests in society by their idleness, and the depredations to which this leads them."

Jefferson had changed. The man who in 1786 spoke of "a bondage, one hour of which is fraught with more misery" than the epoch of tyranny that the American Revolutionaries had recently overthrown, was not the man who in 1814 claimed that American slaves "are better fed . . . , warmer clothed, and labor less than the journeymen or day-laborers of England," living "without want, or the fear of it."

What had happened to the fervent abolitionist who in 1785 could write that "the whole commerce between master and slave is a perpetual exercise of the most boisterous passions, the most unremitting despotism on the one part, and degrading submissions on the other?" The responsibility of public office offers a partial explanation. Having seen how divisive an issue slavery was through his early efforts to abolish it in Virginia and the West, he grew more cautious and compromising. As president, he even refused to be associated with an antislavery poem on the grounds that while he believed in the "holy" cause that the poet espoused such a limited step toward abolition "would only be disarming myself of influence."

Another factor impeding his abolitionist zeal was that, as much as he detested slavery, he did not wish to see the Union destroyed over this issue. He felt that the revolutionary experiment in republicanism must be preserved. The Missouri Crisis of 1819–20, incited by northern efforts to limit the spread of slavery in the West, struck Jefferson as "a fire bell in the night," that could destroy the nation he had worked so hard to create.

Two events of the late 18th and early 19th centuries also checked his enthusiasm for emancipation. In 1791, black slaves rebelled against their French masters on the Caribbean island of Santo Domingo (now the Dominican Republic and Haiti). For more than a decade, fierce fighting raged, until in 1804 triumphant blacks proclaimed the free and independent nation of Haiti. During the conflict, thousands of whites died or fled to the United States where they told tales of black atrocities. Fear spread through the slaveholding South. President Jefferson refused to recognized the legitimacy of the black regime.

In 1800, four years before the creation of Haiti, a planned slave insurrection, Gabriel's Conspiracy, was uncovered in Virginia, giving Jefferson and other slaveholders the uneasy feeling of sitting on a volcano that might erupt at any moment. Gabriel's Conspiracy tempered Jefferson's enthusiasm for emancipation and virtually destroyed the abolitionist movement in Virginia.

Historically speaking, revolutionary radicalism with its idealistic demands for self-sacrifice, has never proved sustainable over the long haul. With the passage of time, all the Founding Fathers of the American Revolution became more conservative, and, while Jefferson retained more of the Revolutionary fervor of 1776 than most other major leaders, he too in time lost much of his youthful radicalism. Furthermore, as a member of the planter aristocracy, he felt strong loyalties to this elite class. Slavery sustained the comfortable lifestyle of Jefferson and the other great planters and such a privileged position was difficult to give up.

Some scholars have speculated that if it were not for his perpetual indebtedness Jefferson would have freed his slaves. Along with inheriting land and slaves on the death of his father-in-law in 1773, Jefferson also acquired a substantial debt that only increased during the Revolution. By 1796, his debt exceeded 8,500 British pounds, an extremely large amount for that period. Jefferson wrote: "The torment of mind I endure till the moment shall arrive when I owe not a shilling on earth is such really as to render life of little value." He even described his debt as a kind of slavery. Yet if freedom from debt would have allowed Jefferson to free his slaves that time never arrived. His expenditures for such things as remodeling Monticello, lavish entertaining, fine wines, and books always outpaced his income. What minimal economic stability he did achieve depended entirely on slave labor that did the "farming, gardening, manufacturing of nails, coopering, carpentry, masonry, shoemaking, spinning and weaving, housework." In the end, it was Jefferson's monumental debt that forced his heirs to sell his slaves and ultimately to lose Monticello itself.

As years went by, Jefferson talked less about freeing the slaves and more about how well they were treated. Obviously, this was a way of soothing a guilty conscience, but it is worth examining what slave life was like at Monticello. Dictating his memoirs in 1847, Isaac Jefferson, a slave born there, called Jefferson "a mighty good master." Yet in another section of his memoir, he described how a certain Colonel Cary had given him "more whippings than he has fingers and toes. . . . Colonel Cary made freer at Monticello than he did at home; whip anybody." What was the truth of the matter?

Judging from the evidence, Jefferson's slaves were better treated than most of those in bondage. Jefferson made every effort to keep slave families together. On one occasion, he bought the wife of his blacksmith, Moses, when her owner moved to Kentucky. "Nobody feels more strongly than I do," he claimed, "the desire to make all practicable sacrifices to keep man and wife together who have imprudently married out of their respective families." He even offered rewards to slave women "when they take husbands at home."

Slaves of all ages worked at Monticello. In his *Farm Book* Jefferson outlined the childhood of his slaves: "Children till 10 years to serve as nurses. From 10 to 16 the boys make nails, the girls spin. At 16 go into the ground [farm] or learn trades." Even the sick or bedridden were given light work. Nace, an injured slave at Poplar Forest, was assigned to shell corn and to make shoes and baskets until he recovered. The workday ran from dawn to dusk, six days a week. By today's precepts that seems excessive, but at the time it was standard for free laborers as well as slaves.

To inspire increased productivity, Jefferson established an incentive system. Isaac recalled Jefferson giving the boys who worked best in the nail factory "a suit of red or blue; encouraged them mightily." Adult skilled workers sometimes received a percentage of profits. Monticello coopers, for instance, could sell for their own benefit every 33rd flour barrel they made. Slave families also were given their own garden plots and poultry yards to raise goods for their use or to sell.

Edmund Bacon, a Monticello overseer, remembered Jefferson as "always very kind and indulgent to his servants. He would not allow them to be at all overworked, and he would hardly ever allow one of them to be whipped." However, the whip was not absent. With Jefferson away for long periods of time on public service, Monticello and his other lands were run by overseers. Some were cruel. William Smith, a man known as "peevish and too ready to strike," spent four years in Jefferson's employ; as did Gabriel Lilly, who on one occasion whipped a 17-year-old boy three times in one day until he was too injured to "raise his hand to his Head." Even Jefferson sometimes ordered whippings. To set an example for the others, he had the persistent runaway Jame Hubbard "severely flogged in the presence of his old companions." Jefferson also sold disruptive slaves to the deep South so that it would seem to the others that such slaves had been "put out of the way by death."

Surviving accounts, however, suggest that in most instances Jefferson's slaves were both industrious and trustworthy. Since farm labor was limited to certain seasons of the year, most slaves learned skilled trades. In addition to making barrels and nails, slaves became expert carpenters, cabinet-makers, masons, stonecutters, blacksmiths, wheelwrights, shoemakers, spinners, weavers, millers, brewers, glaziers, and painters. Even household servants were taught trades that they could follow during the master's absences. Jefferson's loyal manservant Jupiter became a skilled stonecutter. John Hemings learned woodworking and crafted much of Monticello's beautiful interior woodwork and all of that at Poplar Forest.

Clearly, Jefferson took a paternalistic interest in his slaves and saw them as "children" of his large plantation "family." Compared with most other southern planters, he was kind and indulgent to his slaves and provided well for them. His "people," in turn, were devoted to him. However, it was always a master/servant relationship. Jefferson once described his slaves as "those who labor for my happiness." He never believed blacks to be his equal and unfortunately shared with most white Americans of his age a deep and abiding racial prejudice.

Jefferson's fullest discussion of race appears in his one published book, *Notes on the State of Virginia* (1785). Here, under the guise of scientific observation, he reiterated the biased stereotypes common among whites at the time. As to intelligence, he reported that in reason blacks were "much inferior" to whites. "Never yet could I find that a black had uttered a thought above the level of plain narration; never seen even an elementary trait of painting or sculpture." Although Jefferson personally knew the eminent black mathematician Benjamin Banneker and had read the critically acclaimed black poet Phillis Wheatley, he asserted that no black was capable of "comprehending the investigations of Euclid" or of writing a worthwhile poem.

On the basis of no evidence, Jefferson alleged that blacks "secrete less by the kidneys, and more by the glands of the skin, which gives them a very strong and disagreeable odor." He found blacks "more ardent" than whites, but less capable of tenderness and love. Whites, he judged more beautiful in color, hair and "symmetry of form," and for that reason he avowed that blacks sexually preferred whites. Such a mixing of the races, he claimed, improved "the blacks in body and mind, . . . [and] proves that their inferiority is not the effect merely of their condition of life."

Jefferson himself was accused of such a liaison. On September 1, 1802, James Callender, the disreputable and unscrupulous editor of the Richmond, Virginia, *Recorder*, charged: "It is well known that the man [Thomas Jefferson], whom it delighteth the people to know, keeps, and for many years past has kept, as his concubine, one of his own slaves. Her name is SALLY. . . . By this wench Sally, our president has had several children. . . . The AFRICAN VENUS is said to officiate, as housekeeper at Monticello."

Sally Hemings, the slave in question, had come to Jefferson as part of his inheritance on the death of his father-in-law, John Wayles. She was described as "mighty near white" and probably was Wayles's illegitimate offspring and therefore Jefferson's late wife's half sister. Sally and her siblings and their children were given special treatment at Monticello. They did light household chores and were spared from farm labor. The only slaves freed by Jefferson during his lifetime and in his will (eight in all) were members of the Hemings family, and though Sally was never freed, all her children were.

Callender's allegation that Jefferson was the father of Sally's children was taken up by Federalist politicians and later by abolitionists. They accused the author of the Declaration of Independence of dreaming of freedom "in a slave's embrace." In 1974, one historian, the late Fawn Brodie, tried to substantiate the relationship, and more recently the supposed Sally/Jefferson affair was dramatized in the 1995 Merchant/Ivory film, *Jefferson in Paris*.

In his lifetime, Jefferson bore the vilification without comment. Years after Callender's accusations, Jefferson wrote to a friend: "As to federal slanders, I never wished them to be answered, but by the tenor of my life, half a century of which has been on a theatre at which the public have been spectators, and competent judges of its merit. Their approbation has taught a lesson, useful to the world, that the man who fears no truths has nothing to fear from lies. I should have fancied myself half guilty had I condescended to put pen to paper in refutation of their falsehoods, or drawn to them respect by any notice from myself." Virtually all serious Jefferson scholars take him at his word and suggest that the actual father of Sally's children was Jefferson's nephew Peter Carr.

But whether Jefferson ever had an affair with Sally or any other slave woman scarcely mattered. What did matter was that miscegenation (racial mixing) obviously took place at Monticello. Jefferson lived surrounded by slave children and adults of mixed blood. Yet to his way of thinking, miscegenation, while beneficial to blacks, threatened to adulterate the superior white race. Miscegenation, he wrote, "produces a degradation to which no lover of excellence in the human character can innocently consent." Fear of the sexual amalgamation of the races was nearly universal among whites. This was ironic because on a great many plantations, including Monticello, white men had sexual relations with slave women.

Because of his fears of racial mixing and his conviction that blacks were inferior to whites, Jefferson could never conceive of a society in which free blacks and whites lived peacefully as equals. Consequently, all his plans for emancipating the slaves called for removing black Africans from white America. He even dreaded a possible racial war were not freed blacks returned to Africa or sent to the West Indies. In a memorable quote Jefferson proclaimed: "We have the wolf by the ears, and we can neither hold him, nor safely let him go. Justice is in one scale, and self-preservation in the other."

In the end, Jefferson's various plans to gradually abolish slavery with compensation for the owners and transportation of the freed blacks back to Africa, or somewhere else remote from white America, went nowhere. As Merrill Peterson, the foremost Jefferson biographer of this generation, concluded: "At bottom he did not care enough to sacrifice himself, or even put himself to great inconvenience, for the freedom of slaves, certainly not in the declining years of life."

Thomas Jefferson's record on race and slavery remains his most problematic legacy. Yet one must remember that he was a man of his times, burdened by conflicting goals, fears, and responsibilities. His dilemma was white America's dilemma. He never doubted that slavery was wrong and must eventually cease. "Nothing is more certainly written in the book of fate," he declared, "than that these people are to be free." However, because of his racial bias, he was just as certain that they could not remain in the new republic that he had done so much to create.

Ultimately, however, Jefferson's bequest to the antislavery cause would transcend his personal entanglement in slavery and bind the movement with the Declaration of Independence. Abolitionists throughout the 19th century until the last slave was freed exalted the Declaration of Independence and summoned Thomas Jefferson to bear witness against slavery.

10

THE SAGE OF MONTICELLO

"All my wishes end where I hope my days will end, at Monticello." Throughout his public life, Jefferson yearned for the peace and tranquility of his mountaintop mansion. Returning there in March of 1809 after his retirement from the presidency, he set about to "enjoy a repose to which I have long been a stranger." What Jefferson called repose, however, was a day filled with activity. Describing his routine in a letter to a friend, he wrote: "My mornings are devoted to correspondence. From breakfast to dinner, I am in my shops, my garden, or on horseback among my farms; from dinner to dark, I give to society and recreation with my neighbors and friends; and from candle light to early bedtime, I read."

Domestic life at Monticello, though far from tranquil, resounded with the laughter of children and the talk of family members and guests. Jefferson's last surviving daughter, Martha, and her husband, Thomas Mann Randolph, Jr., had a plantation just a few miles to the east of Monticello. During Jefferson's public life, Martha had made it a point to be at Monticello when her father returned there. Now with Jefferson's final retirement, Martha and her family settled permanently at Monticello, and she took over the direction of the household. At the time, Martha had eight children, ranging in ages from eight months to eighteen years. Ultimately the

Randolphs had 11 children. In 1812, Jefferson became a great-grandfather, and by 1820, he wrote to Maria Cosway, with whom he had resumed corresponding, that he had "about a dozen" great-grandchildren and that he lived "like a patriarch of old."

His grandchildren and great-grandchildren adored the aged Jefferson. As one of them recalled: "Cheerfulness, love, benevolence, wisdom, seemed to animate his whole form. I cannot describe the feelings of veneration, admiration, and love that existed in my heart towards him. I looked upon him as a being too great and good for my comprehension; and yet I felt no fear to approach him, and be taught by him some of the childish sports I delighted in."

In addition to the throng of adoring children, innumerable visitors flocked to Monticello. From all over came "people of wealth, fashion, men in office, professional men, military and civil, lawyers, doctors, Protestant clergymen, Catholic priests, members of Congress, foreign ministers, missionaries, Indian agents, tourists, travellers, artists, strangers, friends." They came to seek out and honor the sage of Monticello. Few if any ex-presidents have been so venerated. Some visitors were dear friends, while others were mere curiosity seekers. But many more came as if on a pilgrimage with Monticello as their Mecca.

Jefferson graciously welcomed all comers. Southern hospitality dictated that no stranger be turned away and, besides, there were no nearby inns to accommodate guests. Edmund Bacon, Jefferson's farm manager, described how several whole families would descend at once, each with their own "carriage and riding horses and servants." One acquaintance from Europe arrived with his family of six and stayed 10 months. On occasion, Martha had to lodge and feed more than 50 guests. Claimed Bacon, "I have killed a fine beef, and it would all be eaten in a day or two."

In addition to guests, Jefferson was deluged with correspondence. More than 1,200 letters arrived yearly. "They are letters of inquiry, for the most part," he noted, "always of good will, sometimes from friends whom I esteem, but much oftener from persons whose names are unknown to me, but written kindly and civilly, and to which therefore, civility requires answers." Jefferson was in the habit of spending a few hours each morning from sunup until breakfast at his desk answering letters.

It was a difficult task, both because of the sheer volume of his correspondence and because his right wrist, injured so long ago in Paris, had grown stiffer and more painful over the years. Often he found it necessary to write "under the whip and spur, from morning to night." "Is this life?" he complained. "At best it is but the life of a mill-horse, who sees no end to his circle but death. To such a life, that of a cabbage is paradise."

However, one correspondent with whom Jefferson relished exchanging letters was his old associate John Adams. Collaborators on the Declaration of Independence, patriots of the Revolution, fellow negotiators in Europe, and leaders of the early Republic, the political divisions of the 1790s strained their once close friendship. The bitterly fought election of 1800 in which Jefferson defeated Adams appeared to have ended it forever. Jefferson was furious that Adams had appointed a number of diehard Federalists to federal judgeships in his last hours in office and then had left Washington in a huff, refusing to attend the victor's inauguration. Adams, for his part, blamed Jefferson for the denigrating newspaper attacks against him during the campaign.

In 1804, Adams's wife, Abigail, sent Jefferson a letter of condolence on the death of his daughter Mary whom the Adamses had befriended as a young girl in London and Paris. A brief exchange of letters between Jefferson and Abigail Adams followed, but the old resentments resurfaced and they closed the correspondence.

Not until 1812, through the mediation of their mutual friend Dr. Benjamin Rush, did these two venerable patriots reconcile their differences and commence one of the most remarkable literary dialogues in American history. Rush had urged these "fellow laborers in erecting the great fabric of American independence" to "embrace each other." On New Year's Day 1812, Adams wrote a short note wishing Jefferson "many happy New Years" and signed, "with a long and sincere Esteem your Friend and Servant John Adams." Jefferson was delighted: "A letter from you calls up recollections very dear to my mind. It carries me back to the times when, beset with difficulties and dangers, we were fellow-laborers in the same cause, struggling for what is most valuable to man, his right of self-government."

Thus began an extraordinary epistolary exchange that would continue almost until the day in 1826 that they both died. Their letters ranged over politics, history, philosophy, science, religion, and psychology. They discussed such specifics as the character of Napoleon Bonaparte and the pronunciation of ancient Greek; they speculated on the origins of Native Americans and the nature of aristocracy. Adams was 77 when the correspondence began in 1812, and Jefferson 69. Both enjoyed good health and their lifelong habits of reading and writing kept their minds alert.

One theme running throughout their correspondence concerned the question of human progress. Was civilization advancing to a higher level of virtue, intelligence, and freedom? Perhaps because of his Puritan New England ancestry, Adams was far more pessimistic than the cheerful Virginian. "Let me ask you, very seriously my friend, Where are now . . . *the perfection and perfectibility* of human nature?" asked Adams. "Where is now, the progress of the human mind? Where is the amelioration of society?"

Although willing to admit short-term setbacks to the cause of liberty, Jefferson remained sanguine that freedom would prevail, though "rivers of blood must yet flow, and years of desolation pass over." "Science," he claimed, "is progressive, and talents and enterprise on the alert." Ultimately, Jefferson pinned his hopes on the shining example of America. Writing to Adams in 1821, he prophesied: "I will not believe our labors are lost. I shall not die without a hope that light and liberty are on steady advance. . . . And even should the cloud of barbarism and despotism again obscure the science and liberties of Europe, this country remains to preserve and restore light and liberty to them. In short, the flames kindled on the 4th of July 1776 have spread over too much of the globe to be extinguished by the feeble engines of despotism; on the contrary they will consume those engines, and all who work them."

Jefferson and Adams never met during the last years of their lives, but letters continued to pass between Monticello and Adams's home in Quincy, Massachusetts, without interruption for 14 years. It was an important friendship both for them individually and for the nation at large. As the years rolled on, the generation of the Founding Fathers passed from the scene. Adams and Jefferson alone remained, the last great patriarchs and symbols of America's revolutionary heritage.

In the aftermath of the War of 1812—the second war with England—a wave of nationalism swept the country and Jefferson's and Adams's fame soared as well. But to the latter's regret, it was the Virginian who stole the limelight. "The mighty Jefferson, by his Declaration of Independence, 4 July 1776, carried away the glory both of the great and the little," Adams lamented. "Such are the caprices of fortune."

In addition to family, friends, and correspondents, Jefferson found time in his later life to accomplish one last great public service—the founding of the University of Virginia. Jefferson had been developing his ideas about a university over many years. While in France he studied various European colleges and was particularly impressed with the universities of Edinburgh in Scotland and Geneva in Switzerland. Convinced of the inadequacy of existing American institutions, he envisioned a university "where every branch of science, useful at this day, may be taught in its highest degree."

Friends of Jefferson introduced a proposal to create a state university in 1806. However, the Virginia legislature defeated this plan. In 1814, five years after his retirement from the presidency, the 71-year-old Jefferson accepted appointment to the board of the Albemarle Academy at Charlottesville, not far from Monticello. The academy had been chartered earlier, but had never been established. Jefferson saw an opportunity to elevate the planned academy into a university, and in 1816, after much politicking, the legislature passed a bill, drafted by Jefferson, converting Albemarle Academy to Central College.

Quickly, Jefferson set to drafting designs for his "academical village," with pavilions to house professors, classrooms, and students. The cornerstone of the first pavilion was laid on October 6, 1817. Yet Central College still lacked public funding. Through friends in the legislature, Jefferson submitted a bill that passed both houses in February 1818, providing funds for the establishment of a state university. This was a limited victory. The appropriations were inadequate and the location of the university undetermined. After much further politicking, however, Jefferson's arguments carried the day and Central College became the state supported University of Virginia.

"This is Mr. Jefferson's scheme," said James Madison. "It is but fair that he should carry it out in his own way." And "carry it out" he did. Indeed, no other American university has so completely reflected the ideas of a single individual as has the University of Virginia. With a new zest for life, the elderly Jefferson plunged ahead. He designed the buildings, surveyed the site, laid out its paths, supervised its plantings, and calculated the amount of brick, stone, and lumber needed. He hired carpenters, bricklayers, and even imported sculptors from Italy. Daily he rode his horse Eagle the four miles down the hill from Monticello to the building site. When not on the grounds, he checked the work's progress through a telescope in his garden.

Architecturally the new university was an absolute triumph (see chapter 8). Educationally, too, Jefferson's university was highly distinctive, unique, and influential. Alone among American and European colleges of that era, the university had no religious affiliation nor any professorship of divinity or religious studies. "This institution will be based on the illimitable freedom of the human mind," asserted Jefferson. "For here we are not afraid to follow truth wherever it may lead, nor to tolerate any error so long as reason is left free to combat it."

Jefferson also introduced for the first time the elective system and the division of the university into distinct departments. As initially established, there were eight departments and students were free to chose courses from any one of them. There were no required courses, nor even a division of students into class levels. Students could take written examinations from a particular department whenever they thought themselves ready. This placed the relationship between students and professors on a voluntary basis and treated students as mature adults.

Although the University of Virginia had departments in such traditional subjects as ancient languages, mathematics, and moral philosophy, Jefferson's plan broke from the classical curricula of the New England colleges by embracing new fields of learning such as modern languages, science, economics, law, and medicine. Jefferson placed a high value on "useful knowledge," proclaiming that "knowledge is of little use, when confined to mere speculation."

Teaching at most American colleges at the time relied on memorization and recitation. Professors assigned students material to read and then expected them to recite that material before the class. With such daily drills and no choice of courses, it is not surprising that student unrest ran rampant. In the early 19th century, student riots kept colleges such as Harvard, Yale, and Princeton in an uproar.

Student dissension would not be a problem at the University of Virginia. In addition to treating students more liberally, Jefferson also mandated that instruction be given by lectures rather than the recitation system. Lectures allowed professors to cover a subject in an intellectually stimulating manner, not as academic drill sergeants.

On March 7, 1825, the University of Virginia officially opened. Jefferson was its first rector and chairman of the board of trustees. He remained active in the affairs of the university to the end of his life, hoping that its influence on "those who are to come after us" would be "salutary and permanent."

The university was Jefferson's dream fulfilled and remains his chief educational legacy. His innovative ideas about higher education such as the separation of education from religion, the elective system, the division of the university into departments, instruction by lecture, and the emphasis on science and useful knowledge would help to shape the modern American university.

In most respects then, life was good for the aged Jefferson. In addition to the excitement of building the university, he was blessed with a loving family, a stimulating correspondent, pleasant country society, the adoration of the nation, and worldwide fame. It had been a life well spent, and but for his debts and the growing infirmities of old age, his happiness would have been complete.

Debt, however, destroyed the serenity of his retirement years. On stepping down from the presidency, Jefferson told a reporter that he was leaving office "with hands as clean as they are empty." In fact, he confided to his daughter Martha that his years as president had added more than $10,000 to his already sizeable debts. All told, he owed about $25,000 at the time of his retirement. He now hoped to pay this off through a strict household economy and more efficient management of his farms. This was not to be. Living expenses at home only increased with the swarms of guests arriving regularly at Monticello and income did not improve. The result was that

Jefferson had to borrow more money simply to pay the interest on his existing debts.

To all appearances, the ex-president remained a wealthy planter. He continued to own some 10,000 acres of land and about 200 slaves. Appearances were deceiving. An inefficient slave-labor system, soil exhaustion, the hazards of pests and bad weather, and a depressed international market undermined the profits of Virginia planters. Lands fell in value and when Jefferson tried to sell land few buyers could be found.

To supplement the uncertain and insufficient income from his farms, he experimented with various manufactures. These too proved disappointing. The nailery continued in operation during his retirement, but difficulties in obtaining iron rod and competition from cheaper British nails kept profits at a minimum.

In 1806, he invested more than $10,000 in a large flour mill. Run by two waterwheels, it was, he claimed, "finished in the best manner with every modern convenience." But the cost of maintenance combined with mismanagement by the individuals to whom Jefferson leased the mill and patent litigation took virtually all the profits. He had somewhat better luck in establishing a small textile factory with four spinning jennies capable of weaving some 2,000 yards of cottons, linens, and woolens yearly. However, since the material was used to clothe his slaves, this was not a money-making endeavor.

In 1814, during the War of 1812, the British set fire to the Capitol, destroying the Library of Congress. Jefferson, desperately in need of money, hit upon a scheme that would ease the burden of his debt, while enriching his country at the same time. He offered to sell his magnificent library of nearly 6,500 books to Congress, explaining that "while it includes what is chiefly valuable in science and literature generally, [it] extends more particularly to whatever belongs to the American statesman." Congress appropriated $23,950, and Jefferson's books became the nucleus of what would become one of the world's finest libraries.

But Jefferson could not live without books. So while he applied three-quarters of the money he received from Congress to pay his most pressing debts, most of the remainder went to purchase books. Before his death he would amass another library of some thousand volumes.

Despite the book sale, indebtedness continued to plague Jefferson. American farmers in most states prospered in the years immediately after the War of 1812 when European markets reopened to U.S. produce. Virginia, however, suffered through two years of severe drought followed by a devastating insect infestation the next year. Indeed, in 1817 Jefferson harvested only enough wheat to seed the next year's crop. Younger Virginians fled to the fertile cotton lands of Alabama and Mississippi, and land prices in the Old Dominion plummeted.

Through additional borrowing, Jefferson survived until the financial panic of 1819 plunged him into utter poverty. Already way over his head in personal debt, in the midst of the panic his friend, the former governor Wilson Cary Nicholas, for whom Jefferson had endorsed two notes for $10,000 each, went bankrupt. This left Jefferson obligated for Nicholas's debt. To make matters worse, Jefferson's health deteriorated. Then in 1826, the final year of his life, his son-in-law Thomas Mann Randolph also declared bankruptcy, leaving Jefferson to provide for all the expenses of his daughter and his unmarried grandchildren.

By this time, Jefferson's debt exceeded $100,000. "I am overwhelmed at the prospect of the situation in which I may leave my family," he wrote to his grandson. "My dear and beloved daughter, the cherished companion of my early life and nurse of my age and her children, rendered as dear to me as if my own from having lived with them from their cradle, left in a comfortless situation hold up to me nothing but future gloom."

In desperation, he appealed to the Virginia legislature for permission to dispose of most of his property by lottery. The legislature acquiesced and lottery tickets were printed. As this was publicized, however, the American public learned of Jefferson's plight and organized a fund-raising drive on his behalf. Thousands of dollars poured in from well-wishers. Thinking this would suffice, the lottery was suspended. Jefferson died with the mistaken belief that Monticello had been saved for Martha and her heirs.

For the usually serene and optimistic Jefferson the last years were burdensome. In the fall of 1818, he became seriously ill for the first time in his life. Although he recovered sufficiently

Portrait of Thomas Jefferson at age 78 by Thomas Sully (American Philosophical Society)

to complete the task of building the University of Virginia, he was never again free from bodily pain. His final major illness, a urinary infection, came on in the spring of 1825, leaving him bedridden for months at a time. In March 1826, sensing that he soon would die, he wrote his last will. Sadly, he had little but his debts to bequeath.

In early April 1826, he mustered sufficient strength to attend the meeting of the Board of Visitors of the university, and in

May he rode again to the university to decide on the final placement of the marble columns of the Rotunda. This was his last public outing.

Late in June, Jefferson received an invitation to join in the Fourth of July celebration of the 50th anniversary of American independence, to be held in Washington. Although he would have loved to attend, his health would not permit such a long journey. But the occasion inspired him to reflect once again on the meaning of the American experiment. In a ringing reaffirmation of the principles of the Declaration of Independence, on June 24 he wrote the last letter of his life:

> All eyes are opened, or opening, to the rights of man. The general spread of the light of science has already laid open to every view the palpable truth, that the mass of mankind has not been born with saddles on their backs, nor a favored few booted and spurred, ready to ride them legitimately, by the grace of God. These are grounds of hope for others. For ourselves, let the annual return of this day forever refresh our recollections of these rights, and an undiminished devotion to them.

On July 1, 1826, Thomas Jefferson, 83, lapsed into unconsciousness. He awakened several times during the next few days and asked if it was yet the Fourth of July. The sage of Monticello died peacefully surrounded by his family in the early afternoon of the 50th anniversary of the Declaration of Independence. Later that memorable afternoon, John Adams also expired. His dying words, "Thomas Jefferson still survives," though not literally true, certainly foretold the future. More than any of the other great Founders, Jefferson lived on in the American spirit as the symbol of liberty, equality, and democracy.

They buried Thomas Jefferson beside his wife in the little hillside graveyard at Monticello. He had left instructions for a plain obelisk of coarse stone to mark his grave and requested that his epitaph be "the following inscription and not a word more":

> Here was buried
> Thomas Jefferson
> Author of the Declaration of American Independence
> of the Statute of Virginia for religious freedom
> and Father of the University of Virginia.

The fact that he had twice been elected and served as the president of the United States he did not think important enough to mention. He explained that "because by these, as testimonials that I have lived, I wish most to be remembered."

SELECTED BIBLIOGRAPHY

Students are strongly encouraged to go directly to Jefferson's writings. Two excellent anthologies are: Adrienne Koch and William Peden, eds., *The Life and Selected Writings of Thomas Jefferson* (New York, Random House, 1944); and Merrill D. Peterson, ed., *The Portable Thomas Jefferson* (New York, Viking, 1975). Jefferson's only book, *Notes on the State of Virginia*, is available in many editions and is well worth reading. More personal and revealing about Jefferson and Virginia is Edwin M. Betts, ed., *Thomas Jefferson's Farm Book* (Charlottesville, University Press of Virginia, 1976). Libraries are recommended to purchase the multivolume *Papers of Thomas Jefferson* (Princeton, Princeton University Press, 1950—). Masterfully edited by Julian P. Boyd, Charles T. Cullen, and John Catanzariti, this collection is indispensable for researchers and serious students of Jefferson.

Jefferson was a voluminous letter writer and reading his letters is a fine way to get to know him. A particularly rewarding collection is Lester J. Cappon, ed., *The Adams-Jefferson Letters* (2 vols., Chapel Hill, University of North Carolina Press, 1959). Also engaging are Edwin M. Betts and James A. Bear, Jr., eds., *The Family Letters of Thomas Jefferson* (Columbia, University of Missouri Press, 1966); and Edward Boykin, ed., *To the Boys and Girls, Being the Delightful, Little-Known Letters of Thomas Jefferson to and from His Children and Grandchildren* (New York, Funk and Wagnalls, 1964).

An excellent introduction to Jefferson's intellectual legacy—in his own words—is Jim Strupp, ed., *Revolution Song: Thomas Jefferson's Legacy* (Summit, New Jersey, Ashland Press, 1992). A very readable recent biography is Willard Sterne Randall, *Thomas Jefferson: A Life* (New York, Henry Holt, 1993). For a shorter look at Jefferson's life, Albert Jay Nock, *Jefferson* (New York, Hill and Wang, 1960 ed.) is recommended. For those wishing to sample the writings of some of the leading contemporary Jefferson scholars, see Peter S. Onuf, ed., *Jeffersonian Legacies* (Charlottesville, University Press of Virginia, 1993).

Libraries would do well to acquire Merrill D. Peterson, *Thomas Jefferson and the New Nation* (New York, Oxford University Press, 1970). This is the definitive single-volume biography and is an excellent reference.

For those needing more comprehensive bibliographies of writings about Jefferson consult Frank Shuffelton's *Thomas Jefferson: A Comprehensive Annotated Bibliography of Writings About Him, 1826–1980* (New York, Garland Publishing, 1983); and Shuffelton's *Thomas Jefferson, 1981–1990: An Annotated Bibliography* (New York, Garland Publishing, 1992).

INDEX

Italic numbers indicate illustrations.